PHILLIP ASHLEY RIX

# For the Love of
# CHOCOLATE

## 80 AT-HOME RECIPES
### FROM A MASTER CHOCOLATIER'S IMAGINATION

*Look, Ma, I made it. This one's for you.*

# Arnettie Rix

December 2, 1955–March 28, 2023

*Art direction by Sabryna Lugge*
*Interior design by Lauren Clulow*
*Interior typesetting by Kait Lamphere*

ISBN 978-1-4002-4454-6 (HC)
ISBN 978-1-4002-4455-3 (epub)

Printed in Malaysia
25 26 27 28 29 PJM 5 4 3 2 1

# Contents

# Foreword

by Jacques Torres
known as "Mr. Chocolate"

I opened Jacques Torres Chocolate in 2000, choosing to focus on handmade, premium-quality chocolate simply because I have always loved it passionately. I had a lot of experience as a pastry chef, but I had no education in business. And yet, I had the drive to succeed and a dream to work for myself. I was involved with every aspect of creating the shop, down to helping to hang lights just minutes before our door opened for the first time. I believed in the shop's potential greatly, but the fact of the matter was that the only thing I was certain of was my knowledge of chocolate. I was determined to be the best premium chocolate maker I could be and then sell it at the lowest price. This is still true today, and 2025 marks our twenty-fifth year!

When we first started Jacques Torres Chocolates, there weren't any chocolate shops in New York (and very few, if any, in the rest of the country) that sold European-style artisan bonbons, truffles, pralines, or other delicacies. Just a handful of high-end French pastry shops with only small selections of chocolate-dipped dried fruits and a few bonbons available only in the winter. While it seemed there was a clear opportunity for my chocolate shop to thrive, we had to educate our customers. I used to hand out small

cups of hot chocolate to people waiting in line, in part to give them something sweet while they waited but also to introduce them to real, French-style hot chocolate, as most of them were used to thin, watery hot chocolate made from sweetened "cocoa."

I didn't know it at the time, but our shop soon became a major part of a world-wide evolution involving premium chocolate. It is so incredible to me to see all the talented people opening shops around the country, and to see driven and creative individuals like Phillip pick up the baton and carry chocolates forward.

Opening a box of chocolates from Phillip is like peering into a jewel box. Each perfect piece is super shiny, glossy, and vibrant. It's hard for words—and even the beautiful pictures in this book—to do them justice. His highly creative flavors that honor his Southern roots while capturing some of the magic of Willy Wonka have clearly wowed his customers and huge fan base. But for a professional, it's his ability to create colors and bring them to life on chocolate that we recognize as being exceptional. This is no easy task, and Phillip is clearly very skilled at it.

> **Opening a box of chocolates from Phillip is like peering into a jewel box.**

Phillip and I share a passion to give joy to others through chocolate and pastry. You will find that enthusiasm for all things chocolate in the pages of this book, and I hope it encourages you to make and enjoy your own creations.

Jacques Torres
*French pastry chef and chocolatier*

# Introduction

## How Chocolate Became My Love Language

**W**hen I'm asked what made me decide to exit a successful sales and marketing career in the corporate world to train myself to become a world-class chocolatier, the words of The Notorious B.I.G. come to mind: "It was all a dream."[1]

I remember that light-bulb moment vividly.

I was in my late twenties, living in Baltimore, Maryland, working in corporate sales for huge companies like FedEx, Apple, and UPS. I had studied chemistry in college, thinking I might go to medical school, but business, and eventually entrepreneurship, was my calling. Relating to people has always come easily to me, along with connecting beyond surface-level interactions. The world of sales seemed like it would be a good fit—and it was, for a while. I moved around to different cities and got to wine and dine with clients from all over the world.

Coming from a family of great cooks who instilled in me a deep, lifelong appreciation for good food, in my travels I expanded my palate by learning about new foods everywhere I went. I became friends with sommeliers, distillers, cheesemongers, and chefs who passed on tips to me that I'd try out on friends at dinner parties or on my family during holiday get-togethers. In the office, I became known as the guy bringing in the crazy brownies or trying out a new chili recipe on the sales team.

> **Traveling has certainly played a major role in the chef, but Memphis is responsible for the man.**

I learned a lot about marketing and sales strategies in those jobs. But I knew being confined to an office wasn't for me. I set my sights on one day starting my own business where I could call my own shots.

One night, I woke up at 3:00 a.m. from the weirdest dream. I was in a Godiva chocolate shop with my mother when my childhood idol, Willy Wonka, showed up. As a kid, I'd read *Charlie and the Chocolate Factory* and watched the movie based on the mad confectioner so many times that I could recite parts of the dialogue by heart. When I woke up from my dream, it struck me: I was going to have my own chocolate factory one day.

And I knew just where I wanted to set up shop: Memphis. They say that home is where the heart is, but it took me leaving for nearly thirteen years to fully appreciate the idea. Living elsewhere and traveling has certainly played a major role in the chef, but Memphis is responsible for the man. There's no substitute for family, friends, and the sense of safety and security you get from being close to your roots.

The second-largest city in Tennessee, with a population of just over 620,000, Memphis is truly the land of opportunity, especially for entrepreneurs. It's the kind of city that prepares you for the world because you get a little—or a lot—of everything, but it's still an easygoing place. It's small enough that people can relate based on what high school you graduated from, but it still has a global appeal due to its deep history, musical legacy, and funky vibe.

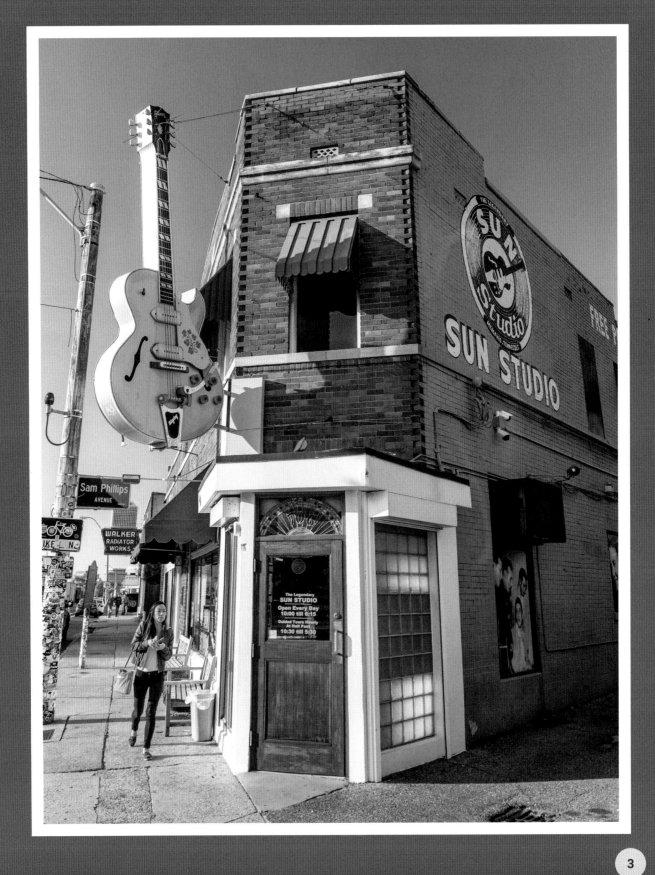

Memphis also provided the foundation for my style of cooking: highly creative and fanciful yet rooted in Southern traditions and culture. Much of what I love most about the South has largely been cultivated by Black men and women like my grandparents and their parents, the foundations laid by the generations of the past and the places that made them who they are. I always carry that awareness with me, and it drives my passion for what I do every day—so much that I get choked up even writing about it.

**Much of what I love most about the South has largely been cultivated by Black men and women like my grandparents and their parents.**

## Made in Memphis

I was born and raised in Memphis, in the Raleigh neighborhood, and spent the majority of my time in the North Memphis community of Hollywood, where my grandmother Jean lived. You could say I was destined to be known for my culinary creativity. I came up in a creative family, and we were always exploring that creativity through playing sports, attending plays, and going to art galleries. But more than anything, my family was, and still is, especially creative in the kitchen. We all liked to cook and loved to eat. My mother ran a medical practice, and my father was a high school basketball coach and history teacher for more than forty years. My grandparents were raised on a sweet potato farm in Arkansas and were big gardeners, and I had aunts and uncles who were painters and generally talented, artistic people.

My mother put that creativity into storytelling too. She made story time a part of my daily routine—at bedtime and beyond. She read anything and everything to me. I've continued to

Memphis also provided the foundation for my style of cooking: highly creative and fanciful yet rooted in Southern traditions and culture.

consume books and movies throughout my life as a result. Fantasy and history are my favorite genres, and both are actively present in the stories I tell with my chocolates.

The first chocolate I ever made for the Phillip Ashley collection—and one of our most popular varieties today—is a perfect example of how I take experiences from the past and present and transform those stories into tangible culinary experiences. The center is made of sweet potato–infused ganache, and the dark chocolate that covers it is dabbed with white edible paint to represent the marshmallows that topped the casserole my grandmother Jean made for every holiday dinner. It just made sense to me to create this chocolate—the first step in my new venture—in honor of the woman who set me on my path to success. It was in Jean's kitchen, when I was very young, where I first felt the sparks of culinary inspiration.

My grandmother Earlean "Jean" Word lived to age one hundred one. We were very close, and even now, years after her passing, I hold her lessons close to my heart and live by them every day. She taught me how to cook, garden, treat people with kindness, and give to those who have less. She would always remind me to "be a pretty boy," her way of saying "be good."

When I was about five years old, I wanted to play with fire—not a good thing for a kid. But instead of shooing me away from her stove, Jean (affectionately called that by everyone, including her grandkids) used it as a teaching opportunity. Showing me basic cooking techniques so I wouldn't get up to trouble without her and risk burning down her house, she, in turn, got a kitchen helper who was by her side when she cooked big family meals.

She let me help her shuck peas, clean greens, make jams, and roll dough for chicken and dumplings. Jean was also a gardening expert and a butcher; she butchered a lot of her own meat out back in the shed. She was an absolute badass. And, in what turned out to be the best thing for me, she let me experiment with unconventional flavor combinations. To this day, I can only eat neck bones with yellow mustard—which some say is strange and others think is just part of my unique palate. (Think about it like putting Dijon mustard on beef Wellington.)

> In what turned out to be the best thing for me, [my grandmother] let me experiment with unconventional flavor combinations.

One of the first things I learned to make was biscuits. I decided to try to "make magic happen" by shaking some hot sauce into the batter. The result was not very magical—or even edible. Jean took one look (and one sniff of the pungent smell) and refused to even touch them. I'm fairly certain, though, that the Cocoa Buttermilk Biscuits I devised many years later (without hot sauce) would have won Jean's seal of approval.

Jean passed away in March 2019. I'm thankful she was around to see me become a chocolatier and got to taste many of my chocolates, including her namesake bonbon (see page 77). She had her ways of letting me know how pleased she was. But she never stopped reminding me to "be a pretty boy," no matter what I was doing.

# Chasing Willy Wonka

The other "person" who inspired me to make magic in the kitchen was Willy Wonka, or at least Gene Wilder's version of the mad candymaker in *Willy Wonka & the Chocolate Factory*. Like my grandmother, he made cooking seem like fun. And in 2007, while contemplating leaving my job in corporate sales in Baltimore, that character reappeared in my life—this time in that strange dream where I ran into him in a chocolate shop.

> The other "person" who inspired me to make magic in the kitchen was Willy Wonka.

The morning after that dream, I awoke with an epiphany that was to be my destiny: I was going to return home to Memphis to become a chocolatier, with the goal of creating the largest portfolio of chocolates in the world. There was one catch: Even though cooking was in my blood, at that point I knew next to nothing about chocolate other than how much I loved to eat a good chocolate bar or my mom's chocolate chip cookies.

I thought about that scene in the movie where Willy Wonka paraphrases a line from Shakespeare and asks, "Where is fancy bred, in the heart or in the head?"[2] I interpreted that quote as asking, "What inspires you to dream, and then leap forward?" To me, the answer comes from both the heart *and* the head. I knew it would take more than passion for me to be successful in my pursuit. I would need my curious mindset to guide me as well.

It's a well-known fact that being a chocolatier is no easy feat. Chocolate demands a level of not only skill but also patience and temperament, with little margin for error. For that reason, many chefs avoid working with chocolate and stay in the "kitchen." Beyond the chocolate factory, however, the industry has been, until very recently, an exclusive club where few gained entry. I vowed to change that.

"Every chocolate should tell a story."
Phillip Ashley

# Designing My "Chocistry" Curriculum

Chocolate-making classes were nearly nonexistent anywhere near Memphis, and books on chocolate technique were overwhelming, complicated, and expensive. But I was hungry for knowledge and determined to accomplish my dream. I drove up to Portland, Maine, for a weekend event where Barry Callebaut chocolate ambassadors were doing a demonstration and showcasing some new equipment. I was able to do a little chocolate making there, and it further fueled my passion for the industry. As I looked around and didn't see anyone who looked like me, I truly felt for the first time that I wanted to make a place for myself in the chocolate world.

I wanted to master every aspect of chocolate so that my work would be taken seriously despite being self-taught. During off-hours from my day job, I delved deep into studying the origins of cocoa, all kinds of ingredients, the human palate, and chemical reactions in foods to help me figure out how to create complementary flavor combinations. I talked to my chef friends and tinkered with recipes in my parents' kitchen. I bought a tiny tempering machine to hold a pound of chocolate and a compressor on eBay to practice airbrush painting on paper plates. Artists like Basquiat, Monet, Jackson Pollock, and Van Gogh were my inspirations and aspirations while turning chocolates into miniature canvases. Their artistic styles were so indicative of who they were, of their personalities and lifestyles. I wanted to use chocolates in the same way, to carve my own path and tell my own story. I was inspired—not just by the art they created but by the way they broke the "rules" to do so.

> Artists like Basquiat, Monet, Jackson Pollock, and Van Gogh were my inspirations and aspirations while turning chocolates into miniature canvases.

Being a huge fan of storytelling in all formats, I wanted to use my ability to connect with people and curate those experiences through chocolate, to master the science so I could create the expressive, edible art I envisioned. My imagination took me to the Inventing Room of Willy Wonka's chocolate factory, where the

## The more unexpected, audacious flavor pairing, the better.

bratty Violet Beauregarde snatches the "Magic Chewing Gum"—a three-course dinner in the form of a stick of gum—from the mad chocolatier's hand and starts chewing it before the kinks have been worked out, causing her to turn blue and swell up like a giant berry when she gets to the final course of blueberry pie.

I made it my mission to capture that stick of gum concept in a chocolate bonbon (but without the nasty side effects). Throughout my journey, my goal has been to shake up traditional chocolate making and create flavor profiles and combinations that surprise and delight. I enjoy a challenge; the more unexpected, audacious flavor pairing, the better.

First came my sweet potato and ganache–filled tribute to Jean, then one in honor of my hometown with hints of barbecue spice. I brought those and other experiments to a fundraiser, and the attendees became my first focus group. Requests began rolling in, and before long I was hosting pop-ups in stores, banks, boutiques, corporate office buildings, and art galleries.

## Chocolate Beginnings

I opened Phillip Ashley Chocolates, a "chocolate studio boutique," in a small storefront in Memphis's lively Cooper-Young district in 2013. This was not your typical candy store by any means. The walls were hung with life-size paintings evoking a French fashion designer's sketchbook, creating a sense of haute couture in the space. My specialty chocolates were displayed like fine jewels in a glass-covered case. Collections were curated and packaged, then sold in elegant black boxes I designed myself, stamped with my handwritten signature in bright-green ink. Besides selling my chocolates at retail, I introduced a specialized gifting program, working with organizations as well as private citizens to customize chocolate designs for special events. I discovered that as much as I enjoyed drawing from my own life experiences for inspiration, the challenge of designing chocolates based on other peoples' stories was just as rewarding.

When ServiceMaster hired me to devise branded chocolates for them, I came up with three flavors—caramel popcorn, strawberry hot sauce, and soy sauce caramel—to represent their first headquarters in Illinois, their current headquarters in Memphis, and their offices in the Philippines, respectively. The chocolates were used in training programs to tell the company's story. And in a nod to Willy Wonka, a ServiceMaster employee won a "golden ticket" to tour my shop and create her own signature flavor.

The closest I've come so far to creating a true "dinner in a bonbon experience" may be The Four Way, named for a historic restaurant in Memphis, an ambitious mash-up of some of the restaurant's soul food specialties. It features a layer of dark chocolate ganache blended with house-made collards, then a layer of white chocolate–cornbread ganache based on my dad's cornbread rec-ipe, all inside a dark chocolate shell. As strange as it may sound, it totally works. I later expanded on that idea for Black History Month with a twelve-piece Soul Food collection with chocolates that include flavors of fried chicken (made with real chicken-skin cracklings), barbecue, mac and cheese, banana pudding, rum cake, and even red Kool-Aid. And, in the spirit of Willy Wonka, I included "golden tickets" in three of the boxes for non-fungible tokens (NFTs) of my Perfect Turtle candy set with access to tastings, exclusive product releases, and future discounts, as well as one "rare" ticket for a monthly chocolate delivery.

I am especially passionate about lifting up Black innovation—something that's long been overlooked in the food and beverage world—and chocolate has been an amazing vehicle for that. I was honored to work with Uncle Nearest Premium Whiskey, a Black-owned spirits company, helping them tell their rich Tennessee history through chocolate. We came up with a collection of twenty-four bonbons infused with their premium aged whiskeys and other ingredients to give them a taste of place—such as the Lincoln County, made with local sugar from maple tree sap and finished with black charcoal salt; and the Queen V, with barrel-aged honey, black tea, cinnamon, and lemon peel made as a tribute to Uncle Nearest's master blender, a descendant of its founder.

> **I'm always thinking about how I can merge the sweet and savory worlds together.**

So much of my work in chocolate really does stem from my Southern roots and Memphis childhood. Growing up, I was used to eating things other kids wouldn't, like rabbit and venison and raw turnips freshly pulled from the ground, and my grandmother gave me permission to experiment with unconventional ingredient combos and learn through making mistakes. I'm  always thinking about how I can merge the sweet and savory worlds together.

That's where my recipe ideas come from.

## A Pandemic . . . and a Pivot

Like businesses everywhere, my company took a big hit during the pandemic. Fortunately, I had started shifting to an almost exclusively online business model right before that first lockdown. Still, we had to get creative. Corporate projects were going away, so I came up with a plan to host a chocolate tasting event via Zoom that I could promote to my online customers and social media followers. I got spirits companies involved as well.

On March 8, 2020, I launched the inaugural Virtual Date Night on Instagram Live. It ended up being a lot of fun, and the fifteen or so guests wanted more. In all, I have hosted more than fifteen hundred virtual chocolate tasting events for more than fifty thousand participants worldwide. It has become one of our most popular service offerings and a way for me to connect with people on a deeper level while exponentially growing my platform.

One huge blessing that came my way during that difficult year was being selected to Oprah's Favorite Things 2020. But with that blessing came a burden. The Oprah effect is real, and I didn't fully realize that until I was waist-deep in orders in what seemed to be the blink of an eye. Within a few hours, we received more orders than we had in the previous eighteen months. It certainly tested my ability to pivot. However, I feel like that—as well as other things we've gone through over the past few years—will continue to help us in the years to come. The lessons have been plentiful. Thankfully, I don't get flustered by challenges. I attribute a lot of that to my parents and having good people around me.

> I began to see possibilities for chocolate greatness in every course of a meal.

Those months in lockdown also gave me more time to play in my kitchen at home, for family dinners and just for fun, so I could show off my creations on Instagram like everyone else in my growing network was doing. I added a pumpernickel-like flavor to sourdough bread with unsweetened cocoa, blew up balloons to make molds for chocolate shells for key lime tarts, chocolatified

**I was reminded of how chocolate is a canvas, and there is a world of ingredients that serve as its palette.**

the Basque cheesecake recipe going viral on the Internet, rubbed ribs with cocoa-spiced barbecue seasoning, and got fancy at cocktail hour with the cacao nibs and chocolate liqueurs lurking in my cabinet. I began to see possibilities for chocolate greatness in every course of a meal, in the way that Willy Wonka perceived a multitude of flavors in a single stick of gum.

Over and over, I was reminded of how chocolate is a canvas, and there is a world of ingredients that serve as its palette. It can send us back in time to a happy place in our memories—or create a new one in our imaginations.

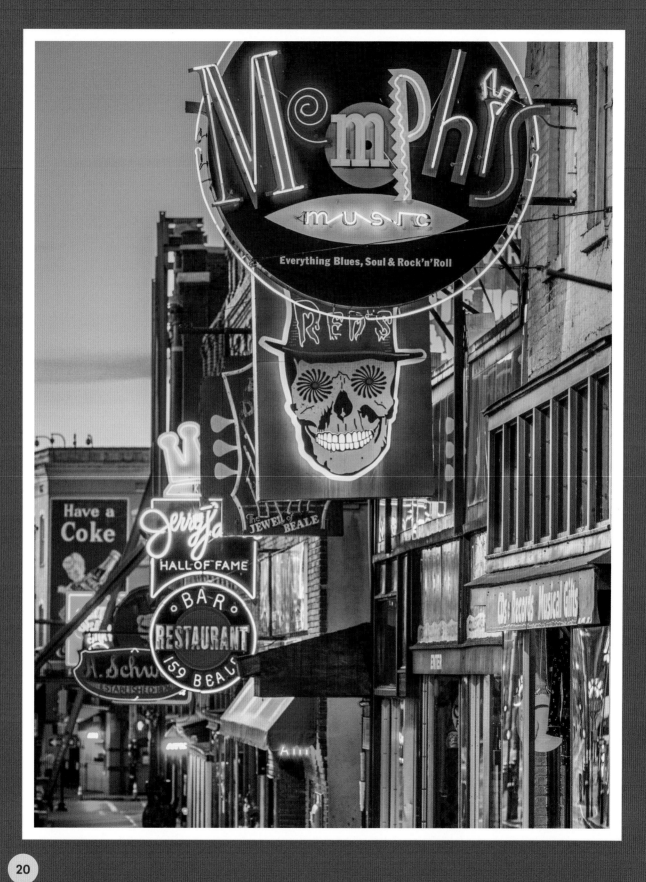

## A Culture of "Thank You"

I have a grand vision for becoming the greatest chocolatier ever. I don't mean simply by making great product but in the impact that I have on the chocolate industry globally and the legacy I leave. In this way, I feel like I'm taking Jean's encouragement and her lessons in my early years—and my family's and mentors' encouragement later on—and carrying them forward in a truly meaningful way.

The level of investment from my family and community allowed me to pursue my dreams, so I try to pay that forward any way I can. As a general principle, I feel it's good to be a giver. I always say kindness is free. If I can help others with the talents and gifts I've been blessed with, I'm all for it. The opportunities I've had are special, and I don't take them for granted. I still remember having to borrow my parents' or my aunt's kitchen because mine wasn't big enough to do even a small job. Each year has brought new opportunities and challenges. I want to continue to get better at meeting those challenges. I want to be least responsible for creating them but most responsible for solving them.

I want the company to thrive so I can continue to provide jobs and a living wage for my employees.

As a part of that overall vision, I am developing a "chocolate campus" in the heart of Memphis that will serve not only as my base of operations but also as an incubator that will develop talented young men and women from all over the world, into future leading chocolatiers who can earn a living wage while gaining valuable culinary and entrepreneurial skills.

> I want to show you how, with a few tricks and the right set of ingredients, you can give yourself a feeling of delicious accomplishment.

I'm a living example of dreaming about something that's completely outside anything you've ever experienced and finding a way to make it your life-changing career. In the pages that follow, I want to show you how, with a few tricks and the right set of ingredients, you can give yourself a feeling of delicious accomplishment—even if it's simply wowing your guests with a great dessert.

## Teaching the "Cocoa Curious"

As it goes with many startups, when I began this business, both my parents helped out quite a bit. My dad was so supportive that when the time came for him to retire from teaching and coaching basketball, he approached me and said he was interested in learning to paint the chocolates. He knew that was the area where I needed help the most because it was hard to find someone who had the discipline and drive to produce like I did. And truth be told, the painting techniques are something even a big kid would find fun—while at the same time yielding beautiful results.

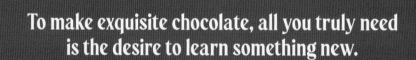

> **To make exquisite chocolate, all you truly need is the desire to learn something new.**

So for a few weeks, I got to be the teacher's teacher. And as my student, my dad proved that by following the methods I've developed, nearly anyone can learn the art of chocolate in less time than some pros would have you believe. He's still my most valuable associate, and now he is passing the skill on to rising apprentices. His experience is also proof that to make exquisite chocolate, all you truly need is the desire to learn something new, even if it challenges everything you've ever done up to that point. Anyone can learn techniques and become successful at creating chocolate that looks and tastes like art.

In Chocistry 101 I've laid out the ingredients and basic tools you'll need to set up a mini chocolate factory on your own kitchen counter. Then you'll learn the most foolproof ways to make ganache, as well as simple tricks for flavoring, dipping, designing, and painting your own custom-designed candies.

In the next chapters, I'll share with you my favorite ways to incorporate chocolate into baked treats, sophisticated desserts, hot drinks, and cocktails. At the end, I'll show you how to work with frostings and glazes to put the "icing on the cake."

I hope that in reading my story and trying my recipes, you'll be inspired to bring some chocolate magic into your kitchen and share it with the ones you love.

# CHAPTER 1

# Chocistry 101

The reason you're holding this book right now is that, when I first became interested in learning about chocolate, I looked around and found . . . almost nothing.

The few books available on *chocistry*—the word I use to describe the art of making high-quality, chocolate-based truffles, bonbons, and other confections—were outdated and didn't fit with modern kitchens or culinary techniques. I started looking around for classes and couldn't find any in Baltimore, where I was living at the time, or in nearby Washington, DC. I expanded my search, and what I discovered is that most of the techniques involved in making truly high-end chocolate are secrets passed down within European chocolate houses. I even looked into enrolling in culinary school, but while you can major in pastry, you can't concentrate solely on chocolate.

But the challenge inspired me. It lit a fire to find out all the techniques being closely guarded by people who definitely don't look like me or share my background, and it motivated me to do things differently, to learn to do them my own way, and to blaze a trail while I was at it.

Today, I'm glad the answers weren't easy to find—because now my dreams and aspirations are bigger than they've ever been before.

I am on a mission. To break boundaries. To empower people. To create community. To tell stories. To celebrate the sweetness in life—one piece of beautiful chocolate at a time. I truly believe that every chocolate tells a story, and that chocolate is a fundamental part of all of our stories.

Chocolate has been such a gift in my life, and I believe its magic can nourish people's hearts and souls and lift them up. I see it every day with my own eyes.

> **Celebrate the sweetness in life—one piece of beautiful chocolate at a time.**

This chapter will cover all the basics of chocistry: what you'll need in your kitchen, how to pick the best ingredients, and the fundamental techniques you'll employ to make truly gourmet chocolates in your home kitchen. My hope is that you'll be inspired to learn something new and then to take what's in this book and infuse into it your own creativity and unique point of view. I truly believe that there's room at this table for all of us.

# Chocolate Terminology: A Glossary of Terms

First things first: Chocistry has its own terminology, which can get confusing if you don't have the basics down. Refer to this glossary if you get stuck on any terminology.

## Couverture

Couverture chocolate contains a higher percentage of cocoa butter than chocolate used in baking or eating—by at least 30 percent. When tempered, couverture chocolate has a glossy sheen and a firm "snap," which is the signature of a fine chocolate confection.

## Dark Chocolate

Rich, velvety dark chocolate[1] is chocolate without any added milk solids. It's characterized by a deeper, sometimes bitter taste. This type of chocolate is composed of anywhere from 30 to 80 percent cocoa. Traditionally, the more cocoa in a bar, the less sugar it will contain and the more bitter it will taste.

## Milk Chocolate

Lighter, sweeter milk chocolate includes milk solids and has anywhere from 10 to 50 percent cocoa content.

## Semisweet or Bittersweet Chocolate

These two terms are sometimes used interchangeably because there is no FDA regulation on the cocoa content of semisweet and bittersweet chocolate. Generally, semisweet chocolate is more bitter than milk chocolate but sweeter than bittersweet and dark chocolate. Semisweet chocolate starts at 35 percent cocoa, and bittersweet ranges from about 35 to 80 percent cocoa.

## Unsweetened Chocolate

Otherwise known as baking chocolate, unsweetened chocolate[2] has no sugar whatsoever. It's made solely from ground cocoa beans. Unsweetened chocolate is useful in baking because it imparts the purest, deepest chocolate flavor and because you have more control over the chocolate-to-sugar ratio in a recipe.

## White Chocolate

Many people will argue that white chocolate[3] isn't actually chocolate, but—humbly speaking—they don't know what they're talking about. White chocolate is chocolate made with cocoa butter rather than cocoa solids.

## Ruby Chocolate

You have to see it to believe it. Ruby chocolate[4] is actually pink. It is derived from ruby cacao plants. This chocolate is about as sweet as white or milk chocolate but has a distinctly fruity, tangy flavor.

## Truffle

Different chocolatiers will use the term *truffle* differently, but in my view, a truffle has a ganache center and is rolled in a topping.

## Bonbon

Like truffles, the definition of *bonbon* can vary, but I describe a bonbon as a molded chocolate shell filled with a ganache, praline, or caramel center.

## Tempering

This is the process of heating and cooling chocolate to specific temperatures to stabilize it for making confections. Tempering creates a smooth and glossy finish and allows chocolate to set for dipped and covered treats that won't melt in your hands.

## Ganache

This concoction is a sweet, creamy mixture of cream and melted chocolate used for fillings or frostings. Other flavorings or ingredients are often added.

## Terroir

This is the distinct flavor that an environment imparts to things grown there. Any edible plant will naturally display characteristics of the soil in which it's grown, the air it absorbs, and the influence of other plants around it. You commonly hear terroir associated with wine, but it's very easy to pick out distinct differences in the terroir of chocolate grown in different countries, including varied tasting notes, color, and eating experience.

## The History of Cocoa: The Ingredient and the Industry

Any journey through the art of cho-cistry should begin with a journey into the past. Cacao has been one of the most coveted ingredients in the world for millennia. Chocolate as we know it today has been delighting people since its invention, but the inception of the chocolate bar occurred only about two hundred years ago. There's a much deeper and richer history, one that began with ancient civilizations in Central and South America, deep in the heart of the rainforest.

The earliest-known consumption of chocolate dates back more than 5,300 years, with the Mayo-Chinchipe culture in present-day Ecuador.[5] Scientists believe the first cacao plants originated in that area of the upper Amazon rainforest and made their way up into Central America by way of migrating peoples.

Throughout almost all its history, chocolate was exclusively a drink, a rarified and sacred beverage. Even the cacao tree's Latin name, *Theobroma cacao*, means "food of the gods."[6] In its earliest iterations, chocolate beverages were made by fermenting the sweet pulp that surrounds the cacao beans in a cacao pod.[7] Today, we'd probably find that version of cacao inedible, as our version of chocolate comes from fermenting and roasting cacao beans, then grinding them and mixing them with sugar and many other ingredients.[8]

But just like us, ancient civilizations like the Olmecs, Mayans, and Aztecs prized cacao, even using it as currency. According to *Smithsonian* magazine, a sixteenth-century Aztec document listed its value: One cacao bean could be traded for a tamale, while one hundred were equal in worth to a "good turkey hen."[9]

**Even the cacao tree's Latin name, *Theobroma cacao*, means "food of the gods."**

The first person outside of Central and South America to encounter cacao was Christopher Columbus, when he found a canoe filled with goods from the Mayans in 1502, including cacao beans for trading.[10]

The reason it was so valuable is that ancient peoples believed it to have spiritual properties. (It's not so far off from how we think about chocolate today. How many times have you heard a truffle described as "heavenly"?) The Mayans and Aztecs worshiped cocoa as a divine gift, using it to brew bitter elixirs that they used in spiritual ceremonies, which they believed granted them vitality and strength. Our word for the thing made from cacao—*chocolate*—comes from the Aztec word *xocoatl*, which described a bitter drink made from cacao beans.[11]

As centuries unfolded, cacao made its grand voyage across the seas to Europe, where it underwent a metamorphosis—from a sacred beverage to an exquisite indulgence. Cacao first reached Europeans through Spanish explorer Hernán Cortés. Aztec king Montezuma II—who himself was believed to have consumed up to fifty cups of xocoatl per day[12]—welcomed the explorer with a banquet that included drinking chocolate, believing Cortés was a reincarnated deity and not a conquistador who would later colonize present-day Mexico as territory of Spain.[13] The Spaniards described the Aztec brew as "a bitter drink for pigs," but when they brought cacao back to Spain in 1528, people began to add honey or sugar to the "brown gold."[14] From there, drinking chocolate, similar to what we enjoy today, quickly became popular.[15]

It wasn't just a sweet indulgence; it was also used as a treatment. Seventeenth-century Europeans used drinking chocolate to aid in illnesses from digestion and mental health issues to heart and kidney disease.[16] At the same time they were importing cacao from "New Spain," as Central America was called after Spain colonized the area, they were taking their medicinal advice from the Mayans and Aztecs. According to *The Journal of Nutrition,* historic documents coming out of New Spain as early as the sixteenth century detailed more than one hundred medicinal uses for cacao.[17]

(Times have changed, but not that much. We now know that chocolate, especially dark chocolate, actually *does* have positive health benefits due to its antioxidant and anti-inflammatory properties. There's even a theory that countries with higher chocolate consumption produce more Nobel laureates because of the confection's ability to enhance cognitive function.[18])

## It wasn't just a sweet indulgence; it was also used as a treatment.

After 5,100 years of enjoying chocolate in essentially one form, a major change occurred. In 1828 Dutch chemist Coenraad van Houten invented the process to make cocoa powder by treating cacao beans with alkaline salts. His "Dutch processing," a term you'll still see today on cocoa powder packaging, turned drinking chocolate from a treat only the rich could enjoy to one that many more people could afford.[19] In 1847 British chocolatier J. S. Fry created the first chocolate bar using sugar, cocoa butter, and chocolate liquor, another substance derived from the cacao plant. Swiss chocolatier Daniel Peter created milk chocolate in 1876 by adding dried milk powder to chocolate, and in 1876 another Swiss chocolatier, Rudolf Lindt, invented a "chocolate conch" machine to mix chocolate and create the smooth consistency that's still a hallmark of Lindt chocolates today.[20]

As innovations in the industry generated more and more demand, the business of chocolate grew larger and harder to manage. Today, about 70 percent of the world's cacao—including what gets shipped to some of the biggest names in chocolate—comes from West Africa, primarily from Ghana and Côte d'Ivoire (the Ivory Coast). But the painful truth about much of that chocolate is that the cacao is grown and harvested using child labor, often with enslaved children who are sold to the cacao plantations or lured there with the promise of education and then trapped with no money and nowhere to turn.[21] According to the Food Empowerment Project, investigators have found widespread child labor on farms in the major African cacao-producing countries, as well as in Brazil, another large producer.[22] Secrecy in the industry and government compliance have helped to hide this ugly side of chocolate. Questionable farming practices have also led to a significant negative impact on the environment, especially regarding deforestation to clear space for new crops, according to the World Wildlife Organization.[23] There's a big disconnect between the joy a simple candy bar can bring you and the reason it costs only one dollar at the grocery store.

But there are absolutely ways to enjoy chocolate without supporting these practices. The simplest is to choose chocolate (and other products, if you can) that are fair trade certified. Sites such as Fairtrade America (www.fairtradeamerica .org), Fair Trade Certified (www.fairtradecertified.org), and Slave Free Chocolate (www.slavefreechocolate.org) list hundreds of brands that sell fair-trade cacao products. A significant amount of ethically sourced chocolate comes from the Ivory Coast, Ecuador, Dominican Republic, and Peru. According to Fair Trade Certified, "Through your purchase of Fair Trade Certified chocolate, millions of dollars have been invested back into cocoa producer communities, resulting in life-transforming projects, such as building schools in the Ivory Coast and improving access to education. Did you know the rate of child labor in cocoa growing communities is significantly lower when the quality of education is higher?"[24]

I consider it my responsibility to be part of the solution when it comes to the problems in the chocolate industry. At Phillip Ashley Chocolates, we exclusively source fair-trade products.

I'm currently working on launching my own line of fair-trade chocolate from Accra and the Kumasi region of Ghana. It's a dream that's going to take a lot of time, but it's a dream I'm making real. My mission is threefold: to advocate for a sustainable cocoa supply chain for West African nations, to educate and train Africans and African Americans in the art and craft of artisan chocolate making, and to make the very best chocolate an approachable luxury.

> I consider it my responsibility to be part of the solution when it comes to the problems in the chocolate industry.

# What Is Couverture? Discovering Various Types of Chocolate

As we delve into the world of chocistry, it's essential to understand the alchemical magic that transpires when cocoa is transformed into chocolate. *Couverture*, a term of French origin, refers to the high-quality chocolate that forms the foundation of everything we create at Phillip Ashley Chocolates. I like to think about that beautiful creation as a symphony orchestra: The cocoa solids, cocoa butter, and sugar all balance in perfect harmony, hitting all the right notes to create a true work of art.

Within this orchestra of flavors, there is an array of chocolate types. White chocolate, delicate and creamy, has no cocoa solids but sings with the melody of cocoa butter. (I defy anyone who says white chocolate isn't "real" chocolate. Tell that to someone who has an out-of-body experience trying one of our transcendent Cherry Blossom White Chocolate Rose truffles.) Semisweet and bittersweet chocolates, with varying levels of sugar, deliver enchanting variations of darkness and sweetness. The whimsical milk chocolate, a universal favorite, strikes the perfect balance between rich cocoa and gentle texture. Blonde chocolate, made by toasting the milk solids before creating white chocolate, has a nutty, caramelized profile. And then there's ruby chocolate, a recent entrant with its natural rosy hue, offering a delicate harmony of fruitiness and depth.

But even in these different types of chocolates, there are endless variations, owing to differences in growing regions. Dark chocolate from the lush rainforests of South America differs from the same product grown on the plains of the Ivory Coast. And then there are the limitless combinations that come from blending and combining chocolates. It's easy to get caught up in the endless—and to me, endlessly fascinating—possibilities of chocolate. Watch out: Once you get started, you just might turn a casual hobby into a life-changing career.

## DIY Chocolate Factory: Essentials for Setting Up Your Home Chocolate Shop

Haute chocolate, whether you're trying it for the first time or learning to make it yourself, can be intimidating. But remember, I started with a couple of outdated books and my tiny kitchen counter. You definitely don't need to be an expert to embark on your chocistry journey. You do, however, want to get a handful of special pieces of equipment:

- lightweight glass or steel mixing bowls
- spatulas, ladles, and whisks
- a palette knife
- a candy thermometer, preferably infrared
- a food scale
- polycarbonate truffle or bonbon molds, enough to make about 36 pieces at a time
- a home chocolate tempering machine, optional (if you want to save time)
- pastry bags
- edible cocoa butter paints, or gold leaf, for decorating
- pastry brush or new paint brushes, for decorating
- an airbrush gun, optional (for decorating)

## Time and Temperature: The Rules and Techniques for Tempering Chocolate

Throughout this book, you'll often see the term "tempered chocolate." It refers to any kind of chocolate that has been through the delicate art of melting and stirring that produces chocolate that shines and snaps. The proper temperature and timing are essential to coax the cocoa butter into crystalline perfection. Tempered chocolate also sets faster, making it easier to work with.

Tempering chocolate using the seeding method is a popular technique to ensure your chocolate looks and tastes the best it possibly can. Seeding helps to encourage the formation of stable cocoa butter crystals in the chocolate, ensuring it has a glossy finish and a satisfying snap when it sets.

Tempering is an essential process in chocolate production. If you're planning on making larger batches of truffles or bonbons, or trying several different recipes, temper a big batch at once and let it cool, then rewarm as much as you need when you need it.

## Chocolate Tempering Chart

Use a candy thermometer along with the chart below as a guide for tempering chocolate using the seeding method.

Tip: When working with dark chocolate, I keep mine around 86.5 to 87 degrees Fahrenheit. And when working with milk chocolate, I generally keep mine at 85 degrees.

|  | Temperature 1: Heat | Temperature 2: Heat |
|---|---|---|
| White Chocolate | 113–122°F | 80–81°F |
| Milk Chocolate | 113–122°F | 84–88°F |
| Ruby Chocolate | 113–122°F | 80–81°F |
| Dark Chocolate | 113–122°F | 86–90°F |

# The Seeding Method

## INSTRUCTIONS

1. If you're starting with bar chocolate, chop it into small pieces. This will help it melt evenly.

2. Melt the chocolate: Set 30 percent of the chocolate aside, as this will be your "seeding" chocolate. Place the other 70 percent of the chocolate in a heatproof bowl. You can use a double boiler or microwave to melt the chocolate gently. If using a microwave, heat the chocolate in short bursts of 15 to 20 seconds, stirring well between each interval to ensure even melting.

3. Check the temperature: Use a candy thermometer to monitor the temperature of the melted chocolate. You want to heat it to around 113 to 122 degrees Fahrenheit (Temperature 1). Be careful not to overheat the chocolate as it can burn easily.

4. Once the chocolate has reached the desired temperature, remove it from the heat source. Add the remaining 30 percent of the chopped chocolate (the seeding chocolate), a third of the remaining weight at a time, to the melted chocolate in the bowl.

5. Use a spatula to stir the chocolate mixture gently until all the seeding chocolate has melted. The temperature should be 90 to 91 degrees Fahrenheit for dark chocolate and 88 to 90 degrees Fahrenheit for milk or white chocolate (Temperature 2).

6. To check if the chocolate is properly tempered, dip the corner of a piece of parchment paper into it, coating it with a small amount of chocolate, or use the back of a spoon. It should set within a few minutes at room temperature, forming a glossy surface with a firm texture. Testing to ensure proper tempering is important; your chocolates will turn out exceptionally well if you do.

7. Once the chocolate is tempered, it's ready to use for dipping, coating, or molding your bonbons and truffles. Work efficiently, as tempered chocolate starts to set relatively quickly at room temperature.

8. If the chocolate starts to thicken or lose its temper while you're working with it, you can gently reheat it in short bursts in the microwave or over a double boiler, being careful not to exceed the desired temperature (90 to 91 degrees Fahrenheit for dark chocolate, and 88 to 90 degrees Fahrenheit for milk, and 80 to 81 degrees Fahrenheit for ruby or white chocolate). A heat gun from your local hardware store also makes a handy tool.

## INGREDIENTS AND EQUIPMENT:

1 pound chocolate (preferably couverture chocolate: bars like Ghirardelli or wafers like Guittard or Valrhona)

thermometer

heatproof bowl

spatula

_____

*A note: Manual tempering can prove to be tricky even for the best of chefs because it relies upon the ambient environment. Things like the kitchen temperature being too high or having too much humidity in the air can really impact the final result. When you're planning to work with chocolate, be sure to lower the temperature of the working area to somewhere between 67 to 70 degrees Fahrenheit at maximum. A few degrees cooler wouldn't hurt, and your chocolate will thank you for it.*

# Preparing Chocolate Molds

Through the years I've found that, of all the types of chocolate molds on the market, polycarbonate molds hold up the best over time and consistently yield the best results. They can be a bit of an investment, but a home chocolatier needs only about three or four molds to start with, depending on the shape you choose and how many pieces are in each mold.

## Prepping the Molds

When you're getting ready to make chocolates, the first thing to do is wash the molds with soap and hot water, using a dishwashing brush to get into the nooks and crannies. Never put them in the dishwasher or they'll warp and become damaged. Dry the molds, then polish them thoroughly with a microfiber polishing cloth. This step is what will ensure you get the glossy luster on the finished product.

## Decorating the Bonbons

Every element of making chocolates is inventive and exciting, but the decoration is where you can truly let your personality and your creativity shine. Will you be decorating treats for a special occasion or a big party? For an exclusive family dinner? To mark a momentous life event? I believe that all of life's moments should be celebrated with chocolate and that chocolates can be a reflection of that memorable time. Later you can go back and re-create those same confections to relive those occasions, bring memories back to life, mark anniversaries, or remind yourself or someone you love of a time of pure joy. Since every chocolate tells a story, I truly hope the recipes and techniques in this book will help you weave many beautiful ones.

Decorating is the first step of the chocolate-making process. The package of edible cocoa butter paint will have warming instructions on it, but generally you'll microwave the container for about twenty seconds, then shake it vigorously to mix. From there, using a knife, a paintbrush, or an airbrush gun,

Watch out: Once you get started, you just might turn a casual hobby into a life-changing career.

spread the color inside the empty mold to create the pattern you want to see. Let the paint dry completely before moving on to the next step.

Don't be afraid to practice this before you start cooking, or to play around to find what works. After my dad retired from teaching, he asked me if he could try his hand at painting my chocolates. Today he's teaching again—only this time, he's teaching our employees how to make beautiful, edible designs. He is our master bonbon artist. Believe me, if he can learn this, so can you.

## Making the Chocolate Shells

The next step is to put chocolate into the molds, to create the shell that will hold the flavored ganache. You definitely want to use tempered chocolate for this. If you skip that step, the finished product will still taste good, but you'll be deeply disappointed with how it looks.

Ladle warm, tempered chocolate into the mold, filling all the individual spaces about two-thirds of the way up the sides. Move the mold around to let gravity fill in the gaps, or use a palette knife to push the chocolate where it needs to go. Gently tap the mold on the counter to release any air bubbles, then invert the mold over your chocolate bowl to let any excess run off, saving that extra chocolate to use later. Using your palette knife, scrape the flat parts of the mold clean and save that chocolate. To double-check that each mold is fully coated with enough chocolate, hold the tray up to the light and look for any spots of light coming through. (If you see any, add a little more chocolate there.) Place to the side at room temperature until fully set—usually about ten minutes if your chocolate is tempered correctly—while you prepare your choice of ganache from one of the recipes in the next chapter.

## Filling and Finishing Chocolate Shells

Once you have your prepared molds and your finished ganache, use a pastry bag to fill each mold. Disposable pastry bags are the easiest to use. Just snip off the tip and place the open pastry bag tip down inside a pint glass with the top folded around the glass's rim. Use a spatula or large spoon to scoop the filling into the bag, leaving several inches at the top. Remove the bag from the glass and twist the wide-top opening closed, squeezing the air out through the bottom. Then squeeze a small amount of ganache into each shell. Leave about one-eighth inch of room in the mold for the chocolate that will be the back or bottom of the bonbon. Tap the tray lightly on the counter to remove any air bubbles. Let the ganache set on the counter or in the refrigerator for several hours.

When it's time to finish the chocolates, rewarm your tempered chocolate in short, thirty-second bursts in the microwave. This method won't affect the temper as long as you don't heat the chocolate over 100 degrees Fahrenheit, so it's important to work slowly and pay attention to the temperature.

Using a small ladle, pour more chocolate over the ganache, using the same method you did to prepare the chocolate shells. Pour in more than you need, spread the chocolate around, tap to remove air bubbles, and scrape the excess melted chocolate back into the bowl to save for later. Refrigerate the bonbons for about twenty minutes, then remove the trays from the refrigerator and invert them gently onto a countertop lined with parchment paper. If they don't come out easily, lightly tap the trays on the counter. If they still don't come out, they need to chill longer. If you break one, don't worry; that's the test piece for quality control.

Once the chocolates are out of the molds, examine them for any little extra edges that you can trim with a paring knife to perfect the finished product. Then package them, plate them, or eat them right away. They're yours to enjoy.

> **If you break one, don't worry; that's the test piece for quality control.**

# CHAPTER 2

# Chocolate by the Bite

## Truffles, Bonbons, and Other Chocolate-Covered Delights

When I first started teaching myself the art of chocolate, I never would have imagined that my creations would one day be served at the Oscars and former President Barack Obama's sixtieth birthday bash, and in homes in big cities and tiny towns around the world.

Okay, who am I kidding? I definitely dreamed they would go that far.

For me, chocolate is more than just an indulgence. It is the medium through which I communicate. I consider myself a storyteller, and chocolate is my love language.

The chocolates in this chapter are some of the first I ever released. They are recipes I developed at home, or I should say in my parents' or my aunt's kitchen because mine wasn't big enough to do even a small order. Today, Phillip Ashley Chocolates is a multimillion-dollar enterprise with a state-of-the-art facility where I pass along my skills to young, enthusiastic people with ambitions of becoming tomorrow's cutting-edge chocolatiers.

In this chapter, you will gain the confidence to create your own designer chocolates as I walk you through mostly short, simple DIY confections that use the full range of chocolate types. There are ganache-based truffles that you'll roll by hand and bonbons you'll paint into molds and fill to make perfect little pieces of art. For a primer on how to temper chocolate and prepare and decorate chocolate molds, refer to chapter 1.

Once you get the basic techniques down, I hope you'll experiment with flavor combinations to create your own signature truffles and bonbons. As I've learned, a little creativity can make a big impression.

## A Few Notes on This Chapter

First, while you can (and definitely should) experiment with flavors, it's important to maintain the stated ratios of solids and liquids in these recipes, and to use heavy cream and golden syrup as stated. Making substitutions will alter the ganache's viscosity, and your chocolates won't turn out well.

Second, recipes for truffles and bonbons are measured using the metric system. I used this system for a couple of reasons. One, chocistry techniques largely come from Europe, where this is their standard measurement system, so most other chocolate recipes utilize it. Two, these recipes call for such small amounts of some ingredients that it's essential to have the precision of measuring in grams. Everything else in this book uses the US customary system you're probably used to, but don't stress about the metric system. Kitchen scales are easy to find and very inexpensive, and they'll do the hard work of converting for you.

The bonbons and truffles can be stored in an airtight container in the refrigerator for up to two weeks. For the best texture and flavor, bring them to room temperature before serving.

# "The Connoisseur" Dark Chocolate Truffles

*Becoming a master chocolatier was a long journey, one that began with this recipe right here. Being able to make a simple ganache became the building block for all my fantastical chocolate creations. That said, a classic, hand-rolled dark chocolate truffle is always a winner and makes for the perfect final bite after a great meal.*

1. Temper the chocolate. See page 39 for instructions. Set 300 grams aside.

2. In a saucepan gently heat the heavy cream over medium heat until just before simmering. Remove the saucepan from the heat, stir in the vanilla, and allow to cool to between 84 and 86 degrees Fahrenheit.

3. In a medium bowl using a rubber spatula, pour the cream into 320 grams of the dark chocolate and stir to combine. Add the golden syrup and continue to stir until well combined and shiny.

4. Place plastic wrap directly on the ganache surface to prevent drying out or a skin forming. Chill in the refrigerator at least 30 minutes.

5. Use a melon baller to scoop out ganache, placing each ball on a cooled baking sheet. Ensure your hands are cool (run them under cold water if necessary, then quickly dry). Roll the balls between your palms to create uniform spheres. Store in the refrigerator while you prep the next steps.

6. When you are ready to dip the truffles, warm the remaining tempered chocolate and allow to cool to between 84 and 86 degrees Fahrenheit. If your chocolate starts to thicken, pop it into the microwave for a few seconds. Many chocolatiers keep a heat gun on hand to blast hot air at the bowl for just a second or two to keep their chocolate the proper temperature.

7. When you're ready to dip the centers, remove from the refrigerator. Working quickly with a fork, roll each ganache center in the dark chocolate. Allow to set briefly but not completely.

8. Place the cocoa powder in a bowl, and roll each ganache ball in the cocoa to coat.

9. Set on a tray lined with parchment paper and allow to fully set. To store, cover with plastic wrap and refrigerate until ready to serve.

**PREP TIME:** 20 minutes, plus chilling time
**COOK TIME:** 10 minutes
**YIELDS:** 36 pieces

620 grams dark chocolate

150 grams heavy cream

5 grams vanilla bean paste, or vanilla extract

25 grams golden syrup, see page 235, or light corn syrup

200 grams unsweetened cocoa powder

# "Thank You Very Much" Peanut Butter and Banana Truffles

*Being from Memphis, where Elvis made Graceland his home, I've been surrounded by the King's influence my whole life. His famous predilection for peanut butter and banana sandwiches inspired this simple truffle. If you're intimidated by molding chocolates, this is a great recipe to try since they are simply hand-rolled in peanuts.*

**PREP TIME:** 30 minutes
**COOK TIME:** 10 minutes
**YIELDS:** 36 pieces

1 medium banana

280 grams dark or bittersweet chocolate

80 grams heavy cream

30 grams smooth peanut butter

30 grams unsalted butter, softened

25 grams golden syrup, see page 235, or light corn syrup

350 grams crushed honey-roasted peanuts

1. Peel the banana and blend in a food processor until smooth. Measure out 60 grams of puree.

2. In a double boiler set over simmering water, melt the dark chocolate and stir until smooth, about 3 to 4 minutes. Remove from heat.

3. While the chocolate is melting, warm the cream, peanut butter, and butter in a small saucepan over medium heat just until small bubbles form on the top, about 5 minutes.

4. Whisk the cream mixture into the melted chocolate to incorporate, then stir in the banana puree and the golden syrup. Stir until well combined.

5. Place plastic wrap directly on the ganache surface to prevent drying out or a skin forming. Chill in the refrigerator overnight.

6. Once set, use a melon baller to scoop out ganache centers.

7. Ensure your hands are cool (run them under cold water if necessary, then quickly dry). Roll the balls between your palms to create uniform spheres.

8. Place crushed peanuts in a medium bowl. Roll each ganache ball in the peanuts to coat.

9. Set on a tray lined with parchment paper, cover with plastic wrap, and refrigerate until ready to serve.

# "Flute" Champagne Truffles

*A little bubbly always makes things better, so I imagine adding more than your normal amount of champagne goodness will make this particular truffle shine. These are hand-rolled, so you don't need molds. Enjoy them with a glass of the good stuff. Cheers!*

1. Temper the milk chocolate, using 100 grams of the dark chocolate for seeding, and allow to cool to between 88 and 90 degrees Fahrenheit. See page 39 for instructions.

2. In a saucepan gently heat the heavy cream over medium heat until just before simmering. Remove the saucepan from the heat and allow to cool to between 84 and 86 degrees Fahrenheit.

3. In a medium bowl using a rubber spatula, pour the cream into the chocolate and stir to combine.

4. Add the champagne and cognac and incorporate fully, then stir in the golden syrup.

5. Place plastic wrap directly on the ganache surface to prevent drying out or a skin forming. Chill in the refrigerator at least 30 minutes, or overnight.

6. Once the champagne mixture is set, use a melon baller to scoop out ganache centers. Ensure your hands are cool (run them under cold water if necessary, then quickly dry). Roll the balls between your palms to create uniform spheres. Store in the refrigerator while you complete the remaining steps.

7. Temper the remaining 300 grams dark chocolate and allow to cool to between 84 and 86 degrees Fahrenheit.

8. Working quickly with a fork, roll each ganache center in the dark chocolate. Allow to set briefly but not completely.

9. Place the confectioners' sugar in a medium bowl. Roll each ganache ball in the sugar to coat.

10. Set on a tray lined with parchment paper and allow to fully set. To store, cover with plastic wrap and refrigerate until ready to serve.

**PREP TIME**: 20 minutes, plus chilling time
**COOK TIME**: 10 minutes
**YIELDS**: 36 pieces

280 grams milk chocolate

400 grams dark chocolate, divided

50 grams heavy cream

50 grams champagne, room temperature

5 grams cognac

25 grams golden syrup, see page 235, or light corn syrup

200 grams confectioners' sugar

# "Nice and Neat" Bourbon Pecan Bonbon

*I really love bourbon and pecans, using the two often when I bake—and sometimes when I cook. This confection is a perfect marriage of two classically Southern flavors. Bring these along for your next family gathering or dinner party, and prepare to be the center of attention!*

**PREP TIME:** 20 minutes, plus setting time
**COOK TIME:** 10 minutes
**YIELDS:** 36 pieces

875 grams dark chocolate, divided

70 grams heavy cream

40 grams bourbon whiskey

25 grams golden syrup, see page 235, or light corn syrup

200 grams chopped roasted, salted pecans

1. Temper all the chocolate. See page 39 for instructions. Using 300 to 350 grams, prepare 36 molds. See page 40 for instructions. Set 300 grams aside.

2. In a small saucepan fitted with a candy thermometer over medium heat, warm the cream to the same temperature as the chocolate, about 84 to 86 degrees Fahrenheit. In a medium bowl pour cream over 225 grams of the tempered chocolate.

3. With a rubber spatula or immersion blender, emulsify chocolate and cream together.

4. Add the bourbon to the chocolate mixture and continue blending, then add the golden syrup.

5. Once fully blended, pour the ganache into a piping bag. Pipe the filling into the molded shells, filling them just to the bottom edge of the opening. Allow to set at room temperature for 10 minutes.

6. If your remaining 300 grams of tempered chocolate has cooled, gently rewarm it in short bursts in the microwave or over a double boiler, taking care not to exceed 86 degrees Fahrenheit. Using a palette knife or a filled piping bag, dab a bit of chocolate on the opening of each bonbon to seal the ganache inside. Allow to set for 15 to 20 minutes in the refrigerator.

7. Remove the bonbons from the molds by gently inverting them onto your workspace. Working quickly, use your fingers and a dipping or regular fork to roll each bonbon in the remaining dark chocolate. Immediately roll each in the chopped pecans. Place on a tray lined with parchment paper and allow to fully set.

# "Key West" Key Lime Pie Bonbon

*My friends, whiskey distillers Susan and Philip Prichard, drove three thousand miles on scooters to get married in Key West, Florida. All that work deserved a special chocolate in their honor. These are a taste of sunshine whenever you need it. They are even better when paired with Prichard's whiskey.*

1. Place the cream in a small bowl, and zest the limes into the cream using a Microplane. Cover and refrigerate overnight.

2. Temper all the chocolate. See page 39 for instructions. Using 300 to 350 grams, prepare 36 spherical molds. See page 40 for instructions. Set 300 grams aside.

3. In a small saucepan fitted with a candy thermometer over medium heat, warm the cream and lime zest to the same temperature as the chocolate, about 88 to 90 degrees Fahrenheit. In a medium bowl, pour cream over 225 grams of the tempered chocolate.

4. With a rubber spatula or immersion blender, emulsify chocolate and cream together.

5. Add mascarpone and cream cheese, and continue blending, followed by the golden syrup.

6. Once fully blended, pour the ganache into a piping bag. Pipe into molded shells, filling them just to the bottom edge of the opening. Allow to set for 10 minutes.

7. Gently rewarm the remaining 300 grams of chocolate in short bursts in the microwave or over a double boiler, taking care not to exceed 86 degrees Fahrenheit. Using a palette knife or a filled piping bag, dab a bit of chocolate on the opening of each bonbon to seal the ganache inside. Allow to set for 15 to 20 minutes in the refrigerator.

8. Remove the bonbons from the molds by gently inverting them onto your workspace. Working quickly, use your fingers and a dipping or regular fork to roll each bonbon center in the remaining white chocolate. Immediately roll each in the graham cracker crumbs. Place on a tray lined with parchment paper and allow to fully set.

---

**PREP TIME:** 20 minutes, overnight steeping, plus setting time
**COOK TIME:** 10 minutes
**YIELDS:** 36 pieces

---

100 grams heavy cream

Zest from two key limes (preferable) or one large lime

875 grams white chocolate, divided

30 grams mascarpone

20 grams cream cheese

25 grams golden syrup, see page 235, or light corn syrup

200 grams graham cracker crumbs

# "Bollywood" Cashew Coconut Curry Bonbons

*When I was growing up, my mom always had coconut around the house. It's a flavor I grew up loving. This molded bonbon combines earthy, rich yellow curry with coconut and cashews for a savory combination inspired by the Indian cuisine I love.*

PREP TIME: 15 minutes, plus time to prepare and decorate the chocolate molds
COOK TIME: 10 minutes
YIELDS: 36 pieces

925 grams milk chocolate, divided

60 grams heavy cream

40 grams coconut milk

8 grams yellow curry powder

20 grams golden syrup, see page 235, or light corn syrup

200 grams finely chopped cashews

1. Temper the chocolate. See page 39 for instructions. Using 300 to 350 grams, prepare 36 spherical molds. See page 40 for instructions. Set 300 grams aside.

2. In a small saucepan fitted with a candy thermometer over medium heat, warm the cream, coconut milk, and curry to the same temperature as the chocolate, about 88 to 90 degrees Fahrenheit. In a medium bowl pour the mixture over 275 grams of the tempered chocolate.

3. With a rubber spatula or immersion blender, emulsify chocolate and cream together.

4. Add the golden syrup and continue blending.

5. Once fully blended, pour the ganache into a piping bag. Pipe into molded shells, filling them just to the bottom edge of the opening. Allow to set for 10 minutes.

6. Gently rewarm your remaining 300 grams of chocolate in short bursts in the microwave or over a double boiler, taking care not to exceed 86 degrees Fahrenheit. Using a palette knife or a filled piping bag, dab a bit of chocolate on the opening of each bonbon to seal the ganache inside. Allow to set for 15 to 20 minutes in the refrigerator.

7. Remove the bonbons from the molds by gently inverting them onto your workspace. Rewarm your remaining chocolate. Working quickly, use your fingers and a dipping or regular fork to roll each bonbon center in the remaining milk chocolate. Immediately roll each bonbon in the chopped cashews. Place on a tray lined with parchment paper and allow to fully set.

# "Sweet Georgia" Amaretto Peach Bonbons

*My grandmother always had peaches in her kitchen and would make unforgettable desserts with them. This bonbon is a tribute to this quintessentially Southern fruit with a sophisticated touch of sweetness from the almond liqueur. In the shop we decorate these with peachy tones to celebrate the fruit inside.*

1. Temper the chocolate. See page 39 for instructions. Using 300 to 350 grams, prepare 36 molds in your choice of shape. See page 40 for instructions. Set 50 grams of tempered chocolate aside.

2. In a small saucepan fitted with a candy thermometer over medium heat, warm the cream to the same temperature as the chocolate, about 88 to 90 degrees Fahrenheit. In a medium bowl pour cream over 250 grams of the tempered chocolate.

3. With a rubber spatula or immersion blender, emulsify chocolate and cream together.

4. Add the almond liqueur and peach preserves and continue blending. Stir in the golden syrup.

5. Once fully blended, pour the peach mixture into a piping bag and tie off. Pipe the filling into molded shells, leaving about ⅛ inch of empty space on the top of each one.

6. Finish the bonbons with the remaining 50 grams of chocolate. Gently rewarm it in short bursts in the microwave or over a double boiler, taking care not to exceed 86 degrees Fahrenheit. Ladle the warm chocolate over the top of the molds. Using a palette knife, scrape the excess chocolate back into your bowl. Bonbons should set within a few minutes at room temperature.

7. To remove from the molds, tap the mold tray gently on a counter, then flip the tray over. If they don't fall out easily, allow the chocolates to set for a few minutes more.

PREP TIME: 15 minutes, plus time to prepare and decorate the chocolate molds
COOK TIME: 10 minutes
YIELDS: 36 pieces

650 grams milk chocolate, divided

75 grams heavy cream

25 grams almond liqueur, such as amaretto

30 grams peach preserves, at room temperature

25 grams golden syrup, see page 235, or light corn syrup

# "Burlesque" Strawberry Cream Bonbons

*One of my earliest cooking memories is of making strawberry shortcake with my mother and asking if we could griddle the biscuits. It was one of my first creative moments in the kitchen, and we all loved the results. (It's a suggestion you might see a little bit later in this book, say, in the breakfast chapter.) This bonbon reminds me of that strawberry shortcake mixed with an ice cream bar—simple, sweet, and nostalgic. Our version uses pink and black paint to evoke the sweet and tart flavor inside.*

PREP TIME: 15 minutes, plus time to prepare and decorate the chocolate molds
COOK TIME: 10 minutes
YIELDS: 36 pieces

5 to 6 large ripe strawberries

625 grams white chocolate, divided

70 grams heavy cream

5 grams vanilla bean paste

20 grams golden syrup, see page 235, or light corn syrup

1. Trim the berries of their stems and hulls, then slice the berries. Puree in a food processor, then strain through a fine sieve, discarding the seeds. Measure out 40 grams of the puree and set aside.

2. Temper the chocolate. See page 39 for instructions. Using 300 to 350 grams, prepare 36 molds in your choice of shape. See page 40 for instructions. Set 50 grams aside.

3. In a small saucepan fitted with a candy thermometer over medium heat, combine the cream and vanilla bean paste. Warm to the same temperature as the chocolate, about 88 to 90 degrees Fahrenheit. In a medium bowl pour cream over 225 grams of the tempered chocolate.

4. With a rubber spatula or immersion blender, emulsify chocolate and cream together.

5. Add the puree and the golden syrup and continue blending.

6. Once blended, pour into a piping bag and tie off. Pipe the filling into molded shells, leaving about ⅛ inch of space on the top of each.

7. Finish the bonbons with the remaining 50 grams of chocolate. Gently rewarm in short bursts in the microwave or over a double boiler, taking care not to exceed 90 degrees Fahrenheit. Ladle the warm chocolate over the top of the molds. Using a palette knife, scrape the excess chocolate back into your stock of melted chocolate. Bonbons should set within a few minutes at room temperature.

8. To remove from the molds, tap the mold tray gently on a counter, then flip the tray over. If they don't fall out easily, allow the chocolates to set for a few minutes more.

# "Porto" Fig Goat Cheese Bonbons

*Believe it or not, this ended up being the confection that gave me the nickname that has inspired my chocolate career. My first-ever collaboration was with Churchill's, a producer of port in Portugal. I made wine-infused chocolates that went to a visitor's center in that country. A writer happened to get some, and all of a sudden Forbes was calling me "the real-life Willy Wonka."[1] We decorate these with a white, black, and crimson palette to mirror the richness of the flavors.*

1. In a medium bowl whisk together the jam, goat cheese, and port wine.

2. Temper the chocolate. See page 39 for instructions. Using 300 to 350 grams, prepare 36 molds in your choice of shape. See page 40 for instructions. Set 50 grams aside.

3. In a small saucepan fitted with a candy thermometer over medium heat, warm the cream to the same temperature as the chocolate, about 100 degrees Fahrenheit. Remove from heat. In a medium bowl pour the cream over 275 grams of the tempered chocolate.

4. With a rubber spatula or immersion blender, emulsify the chocolate and cream together.

5. Add the jam mixture and the golden syrup to the chocolate mixture and continue blending.

6. Once fully blended, pour the ganache into a piping bag and tie off. Pipe the filling into molded shells, leaving about ⅛ inch of empty space on the top of each one.

7. Finish the bonbons with the remaining 50 grams of chocolate. Gently rewarm it in short bursts in the microwave or over a double boiler, taking care not to exceed 86 degrees Fahrenheit. Ladle the warm chocolate over the top of the molds. Using a palette knife, scrape the excess chocolate back into your bowl. Bonbons should set within a few minutes at room temperature.

8. To remove from the molds, tap the mold tray gently on a counter, then flip the tray over. If they don't fall out easily, allow the chocolates to set for a few minutes more.

**PREP TIME:** 15 minutes, plus time to prepare and decorate the chocolate molds
**COOK TIME:** 10 minutes
**YIELDS:** 36 pieces

20 grams fig jam or spread

40 grams goat cheese, room temperature

60 grams ruby port wine

675 grams dark chocolate, divided

125 grams heavy cream

25 grams golden syrup, see page 235, or light corn syrup

# "Lotus Flower" Raspberry Earl Grey Tea Bonbons

*Is there anything better than a hot cup of tea? Yes. These bonbons, which combine the botanical notes of Earl Grey tea with the earthiness of dark chocolate, punched up with the bright, tart acidity of fresh raspberries. In the shop, we splash blue, gold, and bright-red paint on these beauties. Enjoy them with a fresh pot of your favorite brew.*

PREP TIME: 15 minutes, overnight steeping, plus time to prepare and decorate the chocolate molds
COOK TIME: 10 minutes
YIELDS: 36 pieces

130 grams heavy cream

1.5 grams Earl Grey tea leaves

15 to 20 ripe raspberries

625 grams dark chocolate, divided

20 grams golden syrup, see page 235, or light corn syrup

1. In a small container with a lid, pour the cream over the tea, cover, and chill overnight. Strain the cream and discard the tea before using.

2. Puree the raspberries in a food processor, then strain through a fine sieve. Measure out 40 grams of the puree and set aside.

3. Temper the chocolate. See page 39 for instructions. Using 300 to 350 grams, prepare 36 molds in your choice of shape. See page 40 for instructions. Set 50 grams aside.

4. In a small saucepan fitted with a candy thermometer over medium heat, warm the cream to the same temperature as the chocolate, about 100 degrees Fahrenheit. In a medium bowl pour cream over 225 grams of the tempered chocolate.

5. With a rubber spatula or immersion blender, emulsify the chocolate and cream together.

6. Add the puree and the golden syrup and continue blending.

7. Once fully blended, pour into a piping bag and tie off. Pipe the filling into molded shells, leaving about ⅛ inch of empty space on the top of each one.

8. Finish the bonbons with the remaining 50 grams of chocolate. Gently rewarm in short bursts in the microwave or over a double boiler, taking care not to exceed 86 degrees Fahrenheit. Ladle the warm chocolate over the top of the molds. Using a palette knife, scrape the excess chocolate back into your bowl. Bonbons should set within a few minutes at room temperature.

9. To remove from the molds, tap the mold tray gently on a counter, then flip the tray over. If they don't fall out easily, allow the chocolates to set for a few minutes more.

# "Cowboy Chocolate" Tabasco Bonbons

*In "Formation," Beyoncé sings about how she's got hot sauce in her bag.[2] One day we were listening to the song in the kitchen and I thought,* Why not put hot sauce in a truffle? *To everyone's surprise, it worked. This bonbon ended up making its way into the Soul Food Collection we did in honor of Black History Month, which also had flavors like fried chicken, collard greens, and red Kool-Aid—all in chocolate. We decorated our version in red, orange, and yellow paints that looked like flames.*

1. Temper the chocolate. See page 39 for instructions. Using 300 to 350 grams, prepare 36 molds in your choice of shape. See page 40 for instructions. Set 50 grams aside.

2. In a small saucepan fitted with a candy thermometer over medium heat, warm the cream to the same temperature as the chocolate, about 100 degrees Fahrenheit. In a medium bowl pour the cream over 210 grams of the tempered chocolate.

3. With a rubber spatula or immersion blender, emulsify the chocolate and cream together.

4. Add the hot sauce, vanilla bean paste, and golden syrup and continue blending.

5. Once fully blended, pour into a piping bag and tie off. Pipe the filling into molded shells, leaving about ⅛ inch of empty space on the top of each one.

6. Finish the bonbons with the remaining 50 grams of chocolate. Gently rewarm in short bursts in the microwave or over a double boiler, taking care not to exceed 86 degrees Fahrenheit. Ladle the warm chocolate over the top of the molds. Using a palette knife, scrape the excess chocolate back into your bowl. Bonbons should set within a few minutes at room temperature.

7. To remove from the molds, tap the mold tray gently on a counter, then flip the tray over. If they don't fall out easily, allow the chocolates to set for a few minutes more.

---

**PREP TIME:** 15 minutes, plus time to prepare and decorate the chocolate molds
**COOK TIME:** 10 minutes
**YIELDS:** 36 pieces

---

610 grams dark chocolate, divided

135 grams heavy cream

25 grams Tabasco hot sauce

5 grams vanilla bean paste

20 grams golden syrup, see page 235, or light corn syrup

# "Bluff City" Barbecue Bonbon

*Memphis, called "Bluff City" for its location on the bluffs above the Mississippi River, is famous for its barbecue. Walk anywhere in Memphis and you're definitely going to smell something sweet and smoky in the air. The city hosts the World Championship Barbecue Cooking Contest every May, but growing up, my family would grill and smoke meats year-round, whether it was 30 degrees outside or 100 degrees. This chocolate is a nod to my hometown and my family. In the shop we've sometimes decorated this bonbon with the city's seal or in the University of Memphis's signature blue, orange, and gray colors.*

PREP TIME: 15 minutes, plus time to prepare and decorate the chocolate molds
COOK TIME: 10 minutes
YIELDS: 36 pieces

625 grams dark chocolate, divided

90 grams heavy cream

25 grams of your favorite BBQ sauce (Memphis-style, characterized by a sweet, smoky flavor with earthy spices)

5 grams vanilla bean paste

30 grams golden syrup, see page 235, or light corn syrup

1. Temper the chocolate. See page 39 for instructions. Using 300 to 350 grams, prepare 36 molds in your choice of shape. See page 40 for instructions. Set 50 grams aside.

2. In a small saucepan fitted with a candy thermometer over medium heat, warm the cream to the same temperature as the chocolate, about 100 degrees Fahrenheit. In a medium bowl pour the cream over 225 grams of the tempered chocolate.

3. With a rubber spatula or immersion blender, emulsify the chocolate and cream together.

4. Add the barbecue sauce, vanilla bean paste, and golden syrup.

5. Once fully blended, pour into a piping bag and tie off. Pipe the filling into molded shells, leaving about 1/8 inch of empty space on the top of each one.

6. Finish the bonbons with the remaining 50 grams of chocolate. Gently rewarm in short bursts in the microwave or over a double boiler, taking care not to exceed 86 degrees Fahrenheit. Ladle the warm chocolate over the top of the molds. Using a palette knife, scrape the excess chocolate back into your bowl. Bonbons should set within a few minutes at room temperature.

7. To remove from the molds, tap the mold tray gently on a counter, then flip the tray over. If they don't fall out easily, allow the chocolates to set for a few minutes more.

# "Cherry Blossom" White Chocolate Rose Bonbon

*I grew up surrounded by roses. My grandmother was an incredible gardener, and she won awards for her flowers, especially her roses. It's why I have a tattoo of a rose on my hand today, and it's what inspired this chocolate. Feel free to experiment with other flowers and teas to make the botanicals match your favorite memories. In the shop, we paint ours with brown, black, and pink paint to look like branches.*

1. Combine 120 grams of the cream, the rose petals, white tea, and cherries in a small container with a lid. Cover and chill overnight. Strain the cream and discard the solids before using. Stir in the remaining 20 grams heavy cream.

2. Temper the chocolate. See page 39 for instructions. Using 300 to 350 grams, prepare 36 molds in your choice of shape. See page 40 for instructions. Set 50 grams aside.

3. In a small saucepan fitted with a candy thermometer over medium heat, warm the cream to the same temperature as the chocolate, about 100 degrees Fahrenheit. In a medium bowl pour the cream over 240 grams of the tempered chocolate.

4. With a rubber spatula or immersion blender, emulsify the chocolate and cream together.

5. Add the rose water, anise, and golden syrup and continue blending.

6. Once fully blended, pour into a piping bag and tie off. Pipe the filling into molded shells, leaving about 1/8 inch of empty space on the top of each one.

7. Finish the bonbons with the remaining 50 grams of chocolate. Gently rewarm in short bursts in the microwave or over a double boiler, taking care not to exceed 90 degrees Fahrenheit. Ladle the warm chocolate over the top of the molds. Using a palette knife, scrape the excess chocolate back into your bowl. Bonbons should set within a few minutes at room temperature.

8. To remove from the molds, tap the mold tray gently on a counter, then flip the tray over. If they don't fall out easily, allow the chocolates to set for a few minutes more.

---

**PREP TIME**: 15 minutes, overnight steeping, plus time to prepare and decorate the chocolate molds
**COOK TIME**: 10 minutes
**YIELDS**: 36 pieces

---

140 grams heavy cream

10 grams culinary-grade dried rose petals or rosebuds

4 grams silver needle white tea leaves

15 grams sun-dried cherries, roughly chopped

640 grams white chocolate, divided

10 grams rose water

2 grams ground anise

30 grams golden syrup, see page 235, or light corn syrup

# "The Smithsonian" Blueberry, Balsamic, and Black Pepper Bonbon

*Before he retired and became our resident expert in chocolate design, my dad was a history teacher for forty years. This chocolate, named after the spectacular Smithsonian museums in Washington, DC, is a nod to history, when spices like pepper were used as currency. In the past, we've done this bonbon with an argyle print, but now we splash it with white, gold, and navy.*

---

**PREP TIME:** 15 minutes, overnight steeping, plus time to prepare and decorate the chocolate molds
**COOK TIME:** 10 minutes
**YIELDS:** 36 pieces

---

100 grams heavy cream, divided

15 grams black peppercorns, toasted and coarsely ground

20 large blueberries

610 grams dark chocolate, divided

10 grams high-quality aged balsamic vinegar

20 grams golden syrup, see page 235, or light corn syrup

1. In a small container, combine 80 grams of the cream and the peppercorns. Cover and chill overnight. Strain the cream and discard the solids before using. Stir in the remaining heavy cream.

2. Puree the blueberries in a food processor, then strain through a fine sieve. Measure out 25 grams of the puree and set aside.

3. Temper the chocolate. See page 39 for instructions. Using 300 to 350 grams, prepare 36 molds in your choice of shape. See page 40 for instructions. Set 50 grams aside.

4. In a small saucepan fitted with a candy thermometer over medium heat, warm the cream to the same temperature as the chocolate, about 100 degrees Fahrenheit. In a medium bowl pour the cream over 210 grams of the tempered chocolate.

5. With a rubber spatula or immersion blender, emulsify the chocolate and cream together.

6. Add the blueberry puree, balsamic vinegar, and golden syrup.

7. Once fully blended, pour the ganache into a piping bag and tie off. Pipe the filling into molded shells, leaving about ⅛ inch of empty space on the top of each one.

8. Finish the bonbons with the remaining 50 grams of chocolate. Gently rewarm in short bursts in the microwave or over a double boiler, taking care not to exceed 86 degrees Fahrenheit. Ladle the warm chocolate over the top of the molds. Using a palette knife, scrape the excess chocolate back into your bowl. Bonbons should set within a few minutes at room temperature.

9. To remove from the molds, tap the mold tray gently on a counter, then flip the tray over. If they don't fall out easily, allow the chocolates to set for a few minutes more.

# "Mama Jean" Sweet Potato Bonbon

*My grandmother's family owned a sweet potato farm, and she grew them in her backyard, so my family has eaten sweet potatoes in every way you can imagine: roasted, mashed, fried, in sweet potato marshmallow casserole, in pies. We've even baked them into biscuits. This bonbon, though, was the first time any of us had ever eaten them dipped in chocolate. We decorate this one in green and gold, Jean's favorite colors.*

1. Preheat the oven to 400 degrees Fahrenheit, then pierce the potato with a fork all over. Line a baking sheet with foil, then place the potato on the sheet and bake for about 45 minutes, until tender. Allow to cool, then peel and mash.

2. Temper the chocolate. See page 39 for instructions. Using 300 to 350 grams, prepare 36 molds in your choice of shape. See page 40 for instructions. Set 50 grams aside.

3. In a small saucepan fitted with a candy thermometer over medium heat, warm the cream to the same temperature as the chocolate, about 100 degrees Fahrenheit. In a medium bowl pour cream over 200 grams of the tempered chocolate.

4. With a rubber spatula or immersion blender, emulsify the chocolate and cream together.

5. Add the sweet potato, cinnamon, nutmeg, vanilla bean paste, and golden syrup.

6. Once fully blended, pour the ganache into a piping bag and tie off. Pipe the filling into molded shells, leaving about 1/8 inch of empty space on the top of each one.

7. Finish the bonbons with the remaining 50 grams of chocolate. Gently rewarm in short bursts in the microwave or over a double boiler, taking care not to exceed 86 degrees Fahrenheit. Ladle the warm chocolate over the top of the molds. Using a palette knife, scrape the excess chocolate back into your bowl. Bonbons should set within a few minutes at room temperature.

8. To remove from the molds, tap the mold tray gently on a counter, then flip the tray over. If they don't fall out easily, allow the chocolates to set for a few minutes more.

---

**PREP TIME:** 20 minutes, plus time to prepare and decorate the chocolate molds
**COOK TIME:** 55 minutes
**YIELDS:** 36 pieces

---

50 grams mashed sweet potato, from 1 small sweet potato

600 grams milk chocolate, divided

125 grams heavy cream

5 grams ground cinnamon

2 grams ground nutmeg

5 grams vanilla bean paste

40 grams golden syrup, see page 235, or light corn syrup

# "First Take" Banana Dark Rum Bonbon

*This recipe was the first fully composed chocolate bonbon I ever made. One Saturday I thought, You know what? I've been reading about chocolate, I've been studying for a while, let me go whip something up. The results turned out pretty nice—and the rest is history. In the shop we decorate these in black and yellow.*

---

PREP TIME: 15 minutes, plus time to prepare and decorate the chocolate molds
COOK TIME: 10 minutes
YIELDS: 36 pieces

---

### FOR THE BANANA RUM MASH

1 ripe medium banana, peeled and sliced

7 grams unsalted butter

7 grams firmly packed dark brown sugar

25 grams dark rum

1 gram flake salt

### FOR THE BONBONS

400 grams dark chocolate, divided

225 grams white chocolate

80 grams heavy cream

60 grams banana rum mash (from recipe above)

25 grams golden syrup, see page 235, or light corn syrup

1. Place the bananas and butter in a skillet over medium heat. Once the butter begins to melt, add the brown sugar, rum, and salt, and bring to a simmer. When the bananas are soft, begin mashing them together with a fork to incorporate all ingredients. Remove pan from heat and allow to cool.

2. Temper the dark chocolate. See page 39 for instructions. Using 300 to 350 grams, prepare 36 molds in your choice of shape. See page 40 for instructions. Set 50 grams aside.

3. Temper the white chocolate. See page 39 for instructions.

4. In a small saucepan fitted with a candy thermometer over medium heat, warm the cream to the same temperature as the white chocolate, about 88 to 90 degrees Fahrenheit. In a medium bowl pour the cream over the white chocolate.

5. With a rubber spatula or immersion blender, emulsify the white chocolate and cream together.

6. Add the banana rum mash and the golden syrup.

7. Once blended, pour the ganache into a piping bag and tie off. Pipe the filling into molded shells, leaving about ⅛ inch of space on the top of each.

8. Finish the bonbons with the dark chocolate. Gently rewarm in short bursts in the microwave or over a double boiler, taking care not to exceed 86 degrees Fahrenheit. Ladle the warm chocolate over the top of the molds. Using a palette knife, scrape the excess chocolate back into your bowl. Bonbons should set within a few minutes at room temperature.

9. To remove from the molds, tap the mold tray gently on a counter, then flip the tray over. If they don't fall out easily, allow the chocolates to set for a few minutes more.

# CHAPTER 3

# Breads, Brownies, and Bars, Oh My!

**W**riting this chapter was hard. Not because of the writing, but because putting it together brought up so many memories. This chapter, quite honestly, represents where it all began for me—with my mom. My dear mother not only played a major role in raising me, but she was an integral part of my growing into a renowned chocolatier and building a successful business. Finding the words for this chapter evoked a lot of emotions as I reflected on her instruction in my early years—and all my years, really.

As a kid, I spent a lot of time watching classic movies with my mom. Movies certainly played a big role in my vivid imagination. *The Wizard of Oz*, *The Wiz*, *King Kong*, and old black-and-white Shirley Temple movies were some of our favorites. Whenever I think of them, I can almost smell the cookies or cake she, or my grandmother, had baking in the oven while we watched. The baking gene definitely runs in my family, and the desserts in this chapter are part of my life story. Many of these recipes were inspired by my favorite childhood treats—reimagined and elevated with chocolate. With other recipes, you will see my "fancier" side shining through. The good news is, you can have fun with them all!

# Peanut Butter Caramel Cayenne Brownies

*In a very real way, baking brownies began my journey into chocolate. I've always had an adventurous spirit when it comes to cooking, and playing around with different types of brownies was a fun hobby in my early baking days. During my time in corporate sales, I developed a reputation for bringing the results of my new experiments to the office, including this spicy variation. In these brownies, the cayenne pepper delivers a pleasantly unexpected kick that keeps folks coming back for more.*

## PREPARE THE CARAMEL

1. In a small saucepan, heat the cream with the cayenne over medium heat until small bubbles form. Keep hot.

2. In a heavy-bottomed pot, melt the sugar over medium-high heat. Use a paring knife to scrape down the sugar from the sides of the pot, if necessary. Once the sugar begins to melt, turn heat down to low and continue melting. Stir only to break up the sugar.

3. Once all the sugar is dissolved and the caramel is medium amber in color, slowly pour the spicy cream into the caramel, whisking until fully incorporated. (If the sugar recrystallizes, do not panic. Keep stirring and it will remelt.) To ensure there are no remaining clumps of sugar, strain the caramel before proceeding.

4. Add the peanut butter and stir until smooth. Remove from heat and stir in the butter. Allow to cool in refrigerator for 20 minutes.

PREP TIME: 20 minutes, plus chilling time

COOK TIME: 60 minutes

YIELDS: 24

### FOR THE CARAMEL

½ cup heavy cream

¼ teaspoon cayenne pepper (or more if you like a real kick)

½ cup granulated sugar

2 tablespoons smooth peanut butter

½ tablespoon unsalted butter, room temperature

## FOR THE BROWNIES

8 ounces unsweetened chocolate

1 cup (2 sticks) unsalted butter, plus more for greasing

3 large eggs

½ teaspoon salt

1 tablespoon pure vanilla extract

3 cups granulated sugar

1½ cups all-purpose flour

## PREPARE THE BROWNIES

1. In a small saucepan, melt the unsweetened chocolate with the butter over medium heat, stirring frequently until completely melted. Take care not to scorch. Remove from heat and cool.

2. In a stand mixer beat the eggs until light, frothy, and even in color, about 1 minute. Beat in the salt and vanilla.

3. Temper the eggs by adding a small amount of the melted chocolate mixture with the mixer on medium. Add the remaining chocolate to the eggs, then add the sugar.

4. Turn the mixer to low and slowly add the flour until just incorporated.

5. Preheat the oven to 350 degrees Fahrenheit. Grease a 9 × 13-inch baking pan with butter. Pour in half of the brownie batter, tilting the pan to level it.

6. With a tablespoon, spoon half the caramel on top of the batter in two even rows, two inches apart.

7. Pour the remaining batter into the pan and spoon the remaining caramel on top. Drag the tip of a knife through the batter to create a marble effect.

8. Bake for 40 to 45 minutes, or until a toothpick inserted in center comes out clean.

9. Remove from the oven and let cool completely before cutting.

# "Billionaire" Chocolate Praline Shortbread

*My grandmother made incredible shortbread cookies, but just as I do with every treat I dream up, I added chocolate. And caramel. And praline nuts. This take on millionaire's shortbread is so good that I think it's worth even more than a cool million. (Note: This caramel uses the "dry" method and might take you a try or two before you perfect it. For tips on preparation, see Perfect Caramel Sauce, page 224.)*

## PREPARE THE SHORTBREAD

1. Preheat the oven to 325 degrees Fahrenheit. Grease a 9 x 12-inch baking dish and line with parchment paper.

2. In the bowl of a stand mixer fitted with the paddle attachment, mix the butter and sugar on medium until fluffy, about 2 minutes. Reduce speed to low and add the flour and salt. Mix for 1 minute until the mixture is loosely combined.

3. Press the dough into the pan and bake until lightly golden, about 30 minutes. Remove from the oven and allow to cool while you prepare the rest of the components.

## PREPARE THE PRALINE CARAMEL

1. In a heavy-bottomed pot, heat the sugar over high heat. Once it has begun melting, gently move the sugar around to prevent scorching. Do this as little as possible; do not fully stir it.

2. When the sugar has the consistency of wet sand, reduce heat to medium. Continue to move sugar around a bit, breaking up any clumps. Once the sugar is about 90 percent melted, turn off the heat and allow the residual heat to finish, about 2 to 3 minutes.

3. While the sugar is cooking, in a small saucepan over medium heat combine the cream, vanilla bean paste, salt, and corn syrup. Warm the mixture until just before boiling and stir well.

4. Slowly pour the cream mixture into the hot caramel. Only give the sugar about 2 to 3 minutes off the heat before doing this, or it will burn. Let the bubbles settle, then stir with a whisk until well combined. Pour through a strainer to remove any remaining sugar clumps, then stir in the praline nuts.

**PREP TIME**: 15 minutes, plus chilling time
**COOK TIME**: 45 minutes
**YIELDS**: 24 bars

### FOR THE SHORTBREAD

1 cup (2 sticks) unsalted butter, room temperature, plus more for greasing

3/4 cup granulated sugar

1 3/4 cups all-purpose flour

1 teaspoon salt

### FOR THE PRALINE CARAMEL

2 cups granulated sugar

1 cup heavy cream

1 tablespoon vanilla bean paste

1/2 teaspoon kosher salt

1/2 cup light corn syrup

1 cup praline nuts (see page 228)

5. Pour the mixture over the prepared shortbread and smooth the top with a rubber spatula. Chill in the refrigerator for 15 to 20 minutes until set.

## PREPARE THE CHOCOLATE GANACHE

1. In a small saucepan over medium-low heat, combine the chocolate chips and cream. Heat slowly, stirring often, until the chocolate is completely melted and the mixture is smooth and glossy, 3 to 4 minutes.

2. Pour the ganache over the caramel and smooth with a rubber spatula for even coverage. Sprinkle with salt to finish and refrigerate for 15 to 20 minutes to allow the chocolate to set. Serve and store at room temperature.

## FOR THE CHOCOLATE GANACHE

1½ cups dark chocolate chips

⅓ cup heavy cream

½ teaspoon flaked sea salt (I like Maldon)

# Vegan Skillet Brownie with Salted Dark Chocolate Ganache

*I love entertaining, which means hosting people with various diets. This skillet brownie might be plant-based, but it's so chocolatey and indulgent that any chocolate lover will savor it. Even better, it's simple to whip up whenever you're in the mood for a bite of something sweet. Try with a glass of your favorite red wine.*

1. Preheat the oven to 350 degrees Fahrenheit.

2. Prepare the brownies. In a large mixing bowl, mix together the flour, cocoa powder, granulated sugar, brown sugar, baking powder, and salt.

3. In a separate bowl whisk together the vegetable oil, applesauce, nondairy milk, and vanilla.

4. Pour the wet ingredients into the dry ingredients and mix until everything is well combined, then stir in the chocolate chunks.

5. Spray a 10-inch cast-iron skillet with nonstick cooking spray. Pour in the batter and smooth out the top.

6. Bake the brownies for 20 to 25 minutes, or until the top is set and a knife inserted into the center comes out mostly clean.

7. While the brownies are baking, prepare the ganache by melting the dark chocolate chips in a small saucepan over low heat.

8. Once the chocolate has melted, stir in the chopped pecans, nondairy milk, and sea salt until everything is well combined.

9. When the brownies are done, remove them from the oven and let them cool for a few minutes.

10. Pour the ganache over the top of the brownies and spread it out evenly. Serve warm.

---

**PREP TIME:** 10 minutes
**COOK TIME:** 20 to 25 minutes
**YIELDS:** 8 to 10

---

### FOR THE BROWNIES

1 cup all-purpose flour

½ cup unsweetened cocoa powder

½ cup granulated sugar

½ cup firmly packed brown sugar

½ teaspoon baking powder

½ teaspoon salt

½ cup vegetable oil

½ cup unsweetened applesauce

¼ cup oat milk (or other unsweetened nondairy milk)

1 teaspoon vanilla extract

1 cup plant-based chocolate chunks

### FOR THE GANACHE

½ cup plant-based dark chocolate chips

¼ cup chopped pecans

2 tablespoons oat milk (or other unsweetened nondairy milk)

¼ teaspoon sea salt

# Strawberries and Champagne White Chocolate Fudge

*You'll soon discover that I'm all about the bubbly, so I look for any reason to incorporate champagne into a recipe. This one is an elevated take on classic fudge, but with white chocolate to really let the strawberries and champagne flavors shine. Cheers!*

**PREP TIME:** 5 minutes, plus chilling time
**COOK TIME:** 40 minutes
**YIELDS:** 16 squares

1 cup chopped strawberries

2¼ cups granulated sugar, divided

1 cup champagne, divided

½ cup heavy cream

½ cup (1 stick) unsalted butter

1⅓ cups (8 ounces) white chocolate chips

7 ounces marshmallow creme

1 teaspoon vanilla extract

½ cup dried strawberries, loosely crushed (plus more for topping, optional)

1. In a small saucepan combine the fresh strawberries, ¼ cup of the sugar, and ½ cup of the champagne. Cook over medium heat until the fruit has mostly broken down, stirring frequently, about 15 to 20 minutes. Strain out the solids and reserve the strawberry syrup.

2. Line an 8 x 8-inch baking dish with parchment paper.

3. In a large saucepan combine the remaining sugar, champagne, heavy cream, and butter. Cook over medium heat, stirring constantly, until the sugar has dissolved and the mixture comes to a boil.

4. Reduce the heat to low and continue to cook, stirring occasionally, until the mixture reaches 238 degrees Fahrenheit on a candy thermometer, about 10 minutes.

5. Remove the pan from the heat and stir in the white chocolate chips until melted. Stir in the marshmallow creme, vanilla, and dried strawberries until well combined.

6. Pour two-thirds of the mixture into the prepared baking dish and spread it out evenly. Mix the strawberry syrup into the remaining one-third of the fudge, then pour that into the baking dish. Drag a knife through the mixture to make a swirl pattern. Refrigerate for at least 2 hours or until firm. Lift the fudge out of the pan using the parchment paper and cut it into small squares.

# Campfire S'mores Fudge

*I remember my camping days as a kid and how I always loved s'mores. I am a big kid now and like my sweets a tad fancier these days. Think of this dessert as an elevated s'more but one that's ready to eat any time. Instead of allowing to set in a traditional square dish, I like to roll this like a salami, wrap in wax paper, parchment, or plastic wrap, and then slice it when ready to serve. Pair this with a nice glass of bubbly, and you are good to go camping in front of the fireplace—or anywhere!*

1. Place an 8-inch-long piece of plastic wrap on a flat surface.
2. In a large mixing bowl, mix together the graham cracker crumbs, mini marshmallows, dark chocolate chips, and milk chocolate chips.
3. In a medium saucepan over low heat, melt the butter, golden syrup, cocoa powder, sugar, vanilla, and sea salt flakes until fully incorporated, about 5 minutes.
4. Once the mixture is melted and smooth, pour it over the dry ingredients and mix everything together until well combined. You'll still have distinct marshmallow and chocolate pieces in the fudge.
5. Transfer the mixture onto the prepared plastic wrap and shape it into a log. Roll the plastic wrap tightly around the log, twisting the ends to seal.
6. Chill the log in the fridge for at least 2 hours or overnight until firm.
7. Once the log is firm, unwrap it from the plastic and slice. Serve slices dusted with powdered sugar.

PREP TIME: 15 minutes, plus chilling time
COOK TIME: 5 minutes
YIELDS: 12 to 16 slices

6 full sheets graham crackers, crushed into fine crumbs

1¼ cups mini marshmallows

½ cup dark chocolate chips

½ cup milk chocolate chips

½ cup (1 stick) unsalted butter, cubed

¼ cup golden syrup, see page 235, or light corn syrup

½ cup unsweetened cocoa powder

¼ cup granulated sugar

1 teaspoon vanilla extract

¼ teaspoon sea salt flakes

Powdered sugar, to dust

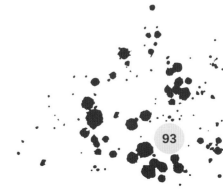

# Simply Perfect Fudge Brownie

*A fancy brownie is an experience, but there's something so appealing about the elegant simplicity of the original. A perfect fudge brownie always hits, whether you're eating it warm from the oven, topped with ice cream, or with your morning coffee for breakfast (no shame in that).*

PREP TIME: 10 minutes

COOK TIME: 40 minutes

YIELDS: 24

1 cup (2 sticks) unsalted butter, plus more for greasing

1 cup dark chocolate chips

1½ cups granulated sugar

2 teapoons vanilla extract

3 large eggs

1½ cups all-purpose flour

½ cup unsweetened cocoa powder

1 teaspoon salt

1 cup semisweet chocolate chips

*Option: Although this fudge brownie is simply perfect as it is, feel free to top with chocolate icing and garnish with chocolate chips for an even more decadent dessert.*

1. Preheat oven to 325 degrees Fahrenheit. Grease an 8 x 10-inch baking pan.

2. In a small saucepan over medium heat, melt the butter and dark chocolate, stirring until fully incorporated. Remove from heat and allow to cool slightly.

3. In a large mixing bowl whisk the butter mixture and sugar together. Add the vanilla and eggs and stir to combine.

4. Add the flour, cocoa powder, salt, and semisweet chips, and stir just until mixed. Transfer to the prepared pan.

5. Bake until a knife inserted into the center of the pan comes out not quite clean but not fully coated in batter, about 40 minutes. Remove from the oven and allow to cool slightly before serving—if you can resist.

# Chocolate Brioche

*Growing up, I would spend part of the summer in Virginia with my Aunt Cleo and Uncle Ron. I remember one summer when she had just bought a brand-new oven and was all about experimenting with baking fresh bread. I became fascinated by both the meticulous process and the delicious results. Over the years brioche has become one of my favorites. I really hope you enjoy this one. It gets no sexier than this elegant bread.*

1. Activate the yeast. In the bowl of a stand mixer, combine 1 cup of the flour, the yeast, and the milk. Stir to fully incorporate, then let sit on the counter for 45 minutes until a few bubbles form.

2. To the bowl add 6 eggs, the remainder of the flour, cocoa powder, sugar, and salt. Fit the mixer with a dough hook, then mix the ingredients on medium speed, for about 1 minute. Increase speed to medium high and knead for 5 minutes. Scrape down the sides of the bowl and knead another 5 minutes, until the dough becomes smooth and elastic.

3. Divide the butter into tablespoons. With the mixer running, add the butter 1 tablespoon at a time, kneading for a full minute between additions to ensure the butter is fully incorporated. (Don't rush this step or your brioche won't turn out.)

4. Once the butter is fully incorporated, knead the dough for another 5 minutes or so. Turn the mixer off and test a small piece of dough. If you can stretch it thin enough to see light through it before it breaks, it's ready. If not, knead another few minutes.

5. Cover the bowl and let the dough rise at room temperature until it has doubled in size, about 1 hour.

6. Grease two 8 x 5-inch loaf pans.

7. Turn the dough out onto a floured surface and punch it down. Divide the dough into 2 equal portions, then divide each of those into 2 sections. Loosely roll out a section of dough into a cylinder about 10 inches long, then repeat with another section. Wrap those 2 sections into a loose braid and place in a loaf pan, ensuring the ends are tucked down into the pan. Repeat with the other half of the dough.

8. Cover the loaves and allow to rise at room temperature until they have doubled in size, about 1 hour, maybe slightly more.

9. Preheat oven to 375 degrees Fahrenheit. Whisk the remaining egg together with the water, then brush the top of each loaf and sprinkle with sugar, if using.

10. Bake for about 25 to 30 minutes, until the internal temperature registers between 190 and 200 degrees Fahrenheit. Allow to rest in the pans for a few minutes before turning out onto a wire rack to cool.

**PREP TIME:** 45 minutes, plus at least 2 hours 45 minutes resting and rising time
**COOK TIME:** 30 minutes
**YIELDS:** 2 loaves

1 (.25-ounce) packet or 2¼ teaspoons active dry yeast (not instant)

3½ cups all-purpose flour, divided

½ cup milk, lukewarm

7 large eggs, room temperature, divided

½ cup unsweetened cocoa powder

½ cup granulated sugar

1 teaspoon kosher salt

1 cup (2 sticks) butter, softened, plus more for greasing

1 tablespoon water

2 tablespoons turbinado sugar, optional

# Blue Cheese Shortbread with White Chocolate Drizzle

*My Savoy truffle—inspired by the Beatles song of the same name and made with blue cheese and white chocolate—always gets a big reaction. People who love blue cheese are an easy sell. They're usually excited to try a confection made with it. I can't tell you how many times someone has told me they typically refuse to eat blue cheese, but they tried the Savoy and it is the only blue cheese they've ever enjoyed. This shortbread is based on that truffle. It pairs sweet, buttery shortbread with savory blue cheese and is finished with a generous drizzle of white chocolate. It might sound strange, but give it a shot. You might be surprised at how much you like it.*

1. Preheat the oven to 325 degrees Fahrenheit.

2. If using granulated sugar, pulse it in a food processor to grind it to a fine consistency.

3. In the bowl of a stand mixer fitted with a paddle attachment, beat the butter and sugar on medium until fluffy, about 1 minute.

4. Add the vanilla and salt to the mixer and mix another 30 seconds.

5. Add half the flour to the mixer, mix for 30 seconds, then add the remaining flour and mix for another minute. The dough will be crumbly.

6. Line a 9 x 13-inch pan with parchment paper, then spread the mixture evenly in the pan. Using the flat bottom of a glass, press the surface fully flat.

7. Bake for 25 minutes, then remove from the oven. Using a sharp paring knife, score the cookies into even bars, about 1 inch by 4½ inches. Using a fork, lightly poke holes across the surface of the dough to vent. Bake another 10 minutes, until lightly golden. Remove from the oven and immediately sprinkle the blue cheese over the shortbread. Remove the cookies from the pan by pulling up the sides of the parchment paper.

8. In a small microwave-safe bowl, melt the white chocolate in 30-second bursts, stirring in between, until melted. Drizzle the chocolate across the top of the shortbread. Using the paring knife, finish cutting the bars while the chocolate is still pliable. Allow to set before serving.

**PREP TIME:** 15 minutes
**COOK TIME:** 40 minutes
**YIELDS:** 24

1 cup caster sugar, or granulated sugar (see step 2)

1 cup (2 sticks) unsalted butter, softened

1 teaspoon vanilla extract

¼ teaspoon salt

2½ cups all-purpose flour

½ cup good quality blue cheese, crumbled (about 2 ounces)

6 ounces white chocolate bars

# Chocolate Butter Pecan Toffee

*Toffee is one of my all-time favorite flavors, and one that goes all the way back to my youngest years, when my grandmother shared her secret stash of Werther's Originals with me. This version has that classic savory-sweet combination but adds a pop of bourbon flavor and a layer of chocolate to finish. If you really wanted to go for it, you could melt a few more cups of chocolate and dip whole pieces of toffee.*

**PREP TIME:** 10 minutes
**COOK TIME:** 25 minutes
**YIELDS:** 8 to 10 pieces

2 cups salted pecan halves, divided

1 cup bourbon-washed butter (see page 237)

1 cup granulated sugar

½ teaspoon salt

1 teaspoon vanilla extract

1 cup milk chocolate chips

*Optional: Add chopped pecans to the top.*

1. Preheat the oven to 350 degrees Fahrenheit. Line a baking sheet with parchment paper. Spread 1½ cups of the pecans on the sheet and toast them in the oven for 5 to 7 minutes, or until fragrant and lightly browned. Remove from the oven and set aside.

2. In a heavy-bottomed saucepan, combine the butter, granulated sugar, and salt. Cook over medium heat, stirring constantly, until the butter is melted and the sugar is dissolved.

3. Attach a candy thermometer to the saucepan. Continue to cook the mixture, stirring frequently, until it reaches 300 degrees Fahrenheit, which is the hard crack stage. This process takes 10 to 15 minutes. Be careful to monitor the temperature closely to prevent burning.

4. Once the mixture reaches the hard crack stage, remove it from the heat and quickly stir in the vanilla and toasted pecans.

5. Immediately pour the hot toffee mixture onto the prepared baking sheet. Use a heatproof spatula to spread the toffee evenly.

6. Sprinkle the milk chocolate chips over the hot toffee. Let them sit for 5 minutes, until they start to melt. Use a spatula to spread the melted chocolate evenly over the toffee. Sprinkle the remaining pecans on top.

7. Allow the toffee to cool completely at room temperature, or place it in the refrigerator to speed up the process. Once it is fully set and hardened, break it into pieces using your hands or a knife. Store the pecan toffee in an airtight container at room temperature. It will keep well for up to 2 weeks.

# White Chocolate Hummingbird Cake Pops with Candied Ginger

*There's no cake more Southern than a traditional hummingbird cake, the rich banana and pineapple confection topped with cream cheese frosting. The beauty of this cake is that every baker has their own version, sometimes adding coconut or even macadamia nuts. My version adds chocolate—of course—and a little kick of ginger to balance out the sweetness.*

## PREPARE THE CAKE

1. Preheat the oven to 350 degrees Fahrenheit.

2. Toast the pecans by spreading them on a baking sheet lined with parchment paper. Bake for 5 to 10 minutes, until nuts are deep brown and fragrant, but keep an eye on them so they don't burn. Remove from the oven.

3. In a mixing bowl combine the flour, baking powder, baking soda, cinnamon, nutmeg, ginger, and salt.

4. In the mixing bowl of a stand mixer fitted with a paddle attachment or a hand mixer, combine the bananas, pineapple, egg, oil, and vanilla. Mix on medium speed to combine, about 1 minute. Add the sugars and mix 1 minute more. Add the dry ingredients and mix until fully incorporated, about 2 minutes.

5. Grease a 9 x 12-inch baking pan, and pour the batter in. Bake for 30 to 33 minutes, until a toothpick inserted into the center comes out clean.

6. Remove from the oven and allow to cool. Using your hands, crumble the cake into a large mixing bowl.

---

**PREP TIME:** 40 minutes, plus chilling time
**COOK TIME:** 45 minutes
**YIELDS:** 24 to 28 cake pops, depending on size

---

### FOR THE HUMMINGBIRD CAKE

½ cup chopped pecans

2 cups all-purpose flour

½ teaspoon baking powder

½ teaspoon baking soda

½ teaspoon ground cinnamon

¼ teaspoon ground nutmeg

¼ teaspoon ground ginger

½ teaspoon salt

1 cup mashed bananas (about 2 medium ripe bananas)

½ cup canned crushed pineapple, with the juice (about 4 ounces)

1 egg

½ cup vegetable oil

1 teaspoon vanilla extract

½ cup firmly packed dark brown sugar

¼ cup granulated sugar

Nonstick cooking spray or butter for greasing

## FOR THE CAKE POPS

4 ounces (½ brick) cream cheese, softened

¼ cup (½ stick) unsalted butter, softened

1½ cups confectioners' sugar

½ teaspoon pure vanilla extract or vanilla bean paste

Pinch of salt

24 ounces white chocolate bars or melting wafers (not chips)

24 lollipop sticks

¼ cup candied ginger, finely minced

## PREPARE THE CAKE POPS

1. In the mixing bowl of a stand mixer fitted with a beater, combine the cream cheese and butter. Mix on high speed until creamy, about 1 minute. Add the sugar, vanilla, and salt. Mix on low to combine, then increase speed to high and mix for 2 minutes, until whipped and smooth.

2. Add to the cake crumbles, and mix to fully combine.

3. Ensure your hands are cool (run them under cold water if you need to) and roll 24 uniform cake balls, about 1½ inches in diameter. Freeze for at least 30 minutes before proceeding.

4. Prepare either a brick of Styrofoam or an empty box that has had small holes poked into it to place the sticks of the cake pops in so they can stand up and preserve their shape while they dry.

5. Melt the white chocolate in 30-second bursts in the microwave, stirring in between, or melt over a double boiler.

6. When the chocolate is melted, remove the cake balls from the refrigerator. Working quickly, smooth the shape into a perfectly round ball, insert a lollipop stick about ¾ inch into the cake ball, and dip it fully into the white chocolate, ensuring the whole surface is covered. Carefully insert the other end of the stick into the box or Styrofoam brick, and sprinkle the top of the cake pop with candied ginger. The cake balls are much easier to handle when cold. You may want to work in batches so they stay chilled. You may also need to rewarm the chocolate.

7. Allow the pops to sit undisturbed for an hour to solidify, either on the countertop or in the refrigerator. Once set, chill in an airtight container in the refrigerator until ready to serve.

**CHAPTER 4**

# The Art of the Chocolate Cookie

O n every level, I am a cookie monster. I even have an apron in the shop with the classic *Sesame Street* character on it. In my mind, there's never a bad time for a perfectly baked chocolate chip cookie. No matter what I'm dreaming up for new confections, it's the treat that I come back to over and over.

The real start of my love of chocolate was my mother's fresh-baked chocolate chip cookies. It was a treat primarily bestowed upon me when I was well-behaved and did something good in school. Maybe that has something to do with why I tended to get good grades! As hard as it is to improve upon that taste memory, it hasn't stopped me from trying. My insatiable curiosity—discovering the world of flavor on my travels—drives me to try to recreate a small piece of that exploration at home, or wherever I might be.

# Perfect Chocolate Chunk Cookie

*If you're a chocolate chip purist, this is the recipe you can go to every day. Everything else in this chapter is fancier and more inventive, but they're all rooted in appreciation for the beautiful simplicity of this cookie. It's my view of what a perfect cookie should be. For the ultimate ice cream sandwich, make these and a batch of Chocolate Mascarpone Gelato (see page 171).*

**PREP TIME:** 10 minutes
**COOK TIME:** 13 minutes
**YIELDS:** 2 dozen cookies

1 cup (2 sticks) unsalted butter, softened

1 cup granulated sugar

1 cup firmly packed light brown sugar

2 large eggs

1 teaspoon vanilla extract

2½ cups all-purpose flour

1 teaspoon baking powder

½ teaspoon baking soda

1 teaspoon salt

1 cup semisweet chocolate chunks

1. Preheat the oven to 375 degrees Fahrenheit. Line two baking sheets with parchment paper.

2. In the bowl of a stand mixer fitted with a paddle, cream together the butter, granulated sugar, and brown sugar for about 2 minutes, until light and fluffy.

3. Add the eggs one at a time, mixing well after each addition. Stir in the vanilla.

4. In a separate bowl, whisk together the flour, baking powder, baking soda, and salt. Gradually add the dry ingredients to the wet ingredients, mixing until just combined.

5. Stir in the chocolate chunks until evenly distributed throughout the dough.

6. Using a tablespoon or your hands, portion dough out into 24 balls, spaced at least 4 inches apart on the baking sheets.

7. Bake for 11 to 13 minutes, or until the edges are golden brown. The centers may still appear slightly undercooked, but they will firm up as they cool.

8. Remove from the oven and let the cookies cool on the baking sheet for 5 minutes, then transfer them to a wire rack to cool completely.

# The Infinity Cookie

*This is the chocolate chip cookie's fancier cousin, the one you bring to a party when you're really trying to show off. In this variation, the dough is formed into oversized cookies and rolled in additional chocolate, then baked until just cooked through so they're soft, chewy, and infinitely delicious.*

1. In the bowl of a stand mixer fitted with a paddle attachment, cream together the butter, granulated sugar, and brown sugar for about 2 minutes, until light and fluffy.

2. Add the egg, sour cream, and vanilla, mixing well.

3. In a separate bowl whisk together the flour, baking powder, baking soda, and salt. Gradually add the dry ingredients to the wet ingredients, mixing until just combined.

4. Stir in the milk chocolate chips until evenly distributed throughout the dough. Chill the dough for at least 30 minutes.

5. Preheat the oven to 375 degrees Fahrenheit. Line two baking sheets with parchment paper.

6. Put the semisweet chips in a small bowl.

7. Scoop the dough into domes using a ¼ cup measuring cup or an ice cream scoop.

8. Roll the tops of each cookie dome in the extra bowl of chocolate chips, making sure you coat them well, and place on the prepared baking sheet, leaving space between each cookie for spreading. Lightly sprinkle each cookie with flaked sea salt.

9. Bake for 12 to 15 minutes, or until the edges are golden brown. The centers may still appear slightly undercooked, but they will firm up as they cool.

10. Remove from the oven and let the cookies cool on the baking sheet for 5 minutes, then transfer them to a wire rack to cool completely.

**PREP TIME:** 10 minutes, plus at least 30 minutes chilling time
**COOK TIME:** 15 minutes
**YIELDS:** 16 cookies

1 cup (2 sticks) unsalted butter, softened

1 cup granulated sugar

1 cup firmly packed light brown sugar

1 large egg

¼ cup sour cream

1 teaspoon vanilla extract

3 cups all-purpose flour

1 teaspoon baking powder

½ teaspoon baking soda

½ teaspoon salt

2 cups milk chocolate chips

2 cups semisweet mini chips

Flaked sea salt, for sprinkling

# Da Grizzness Chocolate Chunk Cookies with Bacon, Pecans, and Brown Butter

*My elevated take on this childhood favorite is full of reminders of my grandparents' quaint home in North Memphis: the smell of country bacon cooking in the mornings, and afternoons filled with picking up pecans from all the trees around the house. Those same memories influenced the flavors in one of my signature chocolates from the Taste of Memphis Collection. The title, "Da Grizzness," is an homage to our basketball team, the Grizzlies.*

---

PREP TIME: 20 minutes, plus
at least 1 hour chilling time
COOK TIME: 15 minutes
YIELDS: 18 cookies

---

1 cup (2 sticks) unsalted butter

½ cup granulated sugar

¾ cup firmly packed
dark brown sugar

2 large eggs

½ cup pure maple syrup

¼ teaspoon freshly
squeezed lemon juice

2¼ cups flour

¾ cup rolled oats

1 teaspoon baking soda

1 teaspoon salt

¼ teaspoon cinnamon

¾ cup dark chocolate chips

¾ cup milk chocolate chunks

¾ cup chopped toasted pecans

4 slices bacon, cooked
and crumbled

1 teaspoon smoked,
flaked sea salt (I like Maldon)

## PREPARE THE BROWN BUTTER

1. In a small skillet over medium heat melt the butter, then reduce heat to medium low. Continue to cook until the butter turns a deep golden brown. Remove from heat and cool to room temperature.

## PREPARE THE COOKIES

1. In the bowl of a stand mixer fitted with a paddle attachment, cream browned butter, granulated sugar, and brown sugar for about 2 minutes, until fully incorporated.

2. Add the eggs one at a time, followed by the maple syrup and lemon juice, continuing to blend until combined.

3. With the mixer on low speed, add the flour, oats, baking soda, salt, and cinnamon and mix until just incorporated.

4. Remove the bowl from the mixer and fold in the chocolate chips and chunks, pecans, and bacon. Cover the dough with plastic wrap and chill in the refrigerator for at least 1 hour.

5. Preheat oven to 350 degrees Fahrenheit. Line two baking sheets with parchment paper.

6. Using a ¼ measuring cup or ice cream scoop, portion the dough onto the baking sheets, leaving room for spreading. Lightly sprinkle each cookie with the smoked salt.

7. Bake for 12 to 15 minutes, or until edges are golden brown and center is still soft. Remove from the oven and let the cookies cool on the baking sheet for 5 minutes, then transfer them to a wire rack to cool completely.

# Dark Chocolate Orange Cookies

*Orange and chocolate is a notorious flavor pairing but not one you often see in cookies (or many other baked goods, for that matter). But it's always been one of my favorite combinations ever since I was a kid and got those foil-wrapped chocolate oranges for Christmas, so I wanted to change that. This cookie combines the richness of dark chocolate with the bright citrus notes of orange. The results are unforgettable.*

1. Macerate the oranges. Place the fruit and liqueur in a container with a lid and let sit about 1 hour.

2. Preheat the oven to 375 degrees Fahrenheit. Line two baking sheets with parchment paper.

3. In the bowl of a stand mixer fitted with a paddle attachment, cream together the butter, granulated sugar, and brown sugar for about 2 minutes, until light and fluffy.

4. Add the eggs one at a time, mixing well after each addition. Stir in the zest and extract.

5. In a separate bowl whisk together the flour, baking powder, baking soda, and salt. Gradually add the dry ingredients to the wet ingredients, mixing until just combined.

6. Stir in the chocolate chips and the macerated orange.

7. Scoop ¼ cup of the dough into domes using a measuring cup or ice cream scoop and place on the pan, leaving room for spreading.

8. Bake for 12 to 15 minutes, or until the edges are golden brown. The centers may still appear slightly undercooked, but they will firm up as they cool.

9. Remove from the oven and let the cookies cool on the baking sheet for 5 minutes, then transfer them to a wire rack to cool completely.

PREP TIME: 10 minutes
COOK TIME: 15 minutes
YIELDS: 2 dozen cookies

3 ounces finely chopped dried orange slices

¼ cup orange brandy liqueur (I like Grand Marnier)

1 cup (2 sticks) unsalted butter, softened

1 cup granulated sugar

½ cup firmly packed light brown sugar

2 large eggs

Zest of 1 large orange

1 teaspoon orange extract

2¾ cups all-purpose flour

1 teaspoon baking powder

½ teaspoon baking soda

1 teaspoon salt

1 cup dark chocolate chips

# Chocolate Sandwich Cookies with Peanut Butter Mousse

*When I was growing up, Tagalong Girl Scout Cookies were something I looked forward to every year. What's not to love about a peanut butter and chocolate cookie? My mom always kept them in the kitchen during Girl Scout Cookie season, along with Samoas and Thin Mints. In this version I've swapped the traditional chocolate coating for chocolate cookies that sandwich luxe peanut butter filling, but if you wanted to dip the finished product in chocolate, well, I wouldn't blame you.*

**PREP TIME:** 30 minutes, plus at least 1 hour chilling time
**COOK TIME:** 14 minutes
**YIELDS:** 20 sandwiches

## FOR THE CHOCOLATE COOKIES

½ cup (1 stick) unsalted butter, softened

½ cup granulated sugar

½ cup firmly packed dark brown sugar

2 large eggs

1 teaspoon vanilla extract

1 cup all-purpose flour

⅔ cup unsweetened cocoa powder

1 teaspoon baking soda

½ teaspoon salt

1½ cups dark chocolate chips

## FOR THE PEANUT BUTTER MOUSSE

½ cup (1 stick) unsalted butter, softened

4 ounces cream cheese, softened

½ cup creamy peanut butter

½ cup confectioners' sugar

### PREPARE THE COOKIES

1. In the bowl of a stand mixer fitted with the paddle attachment, cream the butter, granulated sugar, and brown sugar on medium until light and fluffy, about 2 minutes.

2. Add the eggs and vanilla and mix another minute.

3. In a medium mixing bowl, combine the flour, cocoa powder, baking soda, and salt. With the mixer on low, slowly incorporate the dry ingredients, then the chocolate chips.

4. Cover and refrigerate dough for at least 1 hour.

5. Preheat oven to 350 degrees Fahrenheit. Line 2 baking sheets with parchment paper.

6. Using a tablespoon, portion out each cookie, rolling each into a ball. There should be about 40 balls.

7. Space dough ball evenly on the baking sheets, leaving space for spreading. Bake 12 to 14 minutes, until the edges are baked and the centers are still slightly soft.

### PREPARE THE MOUSSE

1. In the bowl of a stand mixer fitted with a balloon whip, cream the butter, cream cheese, and peanut butter together until light and fluffy, about 2 minutes.

2. Slowly add the sugar and mix another minute, until fully combined. Refrigerate until cookies are completely cool.

3. Transfer the mousse to a piping bag. Pipe the mousse onto the flat side of 20 of the cookies and top with the remaining cookies, flat side down. Refrigerate until ready to serve.

# Dinner Party Cheesecake-Stuffed Cookies

*Cheesecake can be made any time of year, but these cookies—with walnuts, cranberries, dark chocolate, and a luxe cheesecake filling—truly feel like a special occasion. Serve them at a dinner party, or bring them to a holiday celebration to instantly become the favorite relative or friend.*

## PREPARE THE CHEESECAKE

1. In the bowl of a stand mixer fitted with a paddle attachment, cream together the cream cheese, sugar, and salt until light and fluffy, about 2 minutes. Add the vanilla and mix another 30 seconds.

2. On a baking sheet lined with parchment paper, portion out tablespoons of the cheese mixture into rounded mounds. Freeze for at least 20 minutes.

## PREPARE THE COOKIES

1. In the bowl of a stand mixer fitted with a paddle attachment, cream together the butter, granulated sugar, and brown sugar until light and fluffy, about 2 minutes.

2. Add the eggs one at a time, then the vanilla.

3. In a separate bowl whisk together the flour, baking powder, baking soda, and salt. Gradually add the dry ingredients to the wet ingredients, mixing until just combined.

4. Stir in the chocolate chips, cranberries, and walnuts.

5. Line two baking sheets with parchment paper. Scoop ¼ cup of dough using a measuring cup or ice cream scoop, then flatten it into a disc. Place a frozen cheesecake in the center, then wrap the dough full around it to seal. Place on cookie sheet, leaving space for spreading. Remove only a few frozen pieces of cheesecake at a time, as they will melt quickly. Once they're all fully assembled, freeze the cookies for at least 20 minutes before baking.

6. Preheat the oven to 375 degrees Fahrenheit. Bake for 16 to 17 minutes, or until the edges are golden brown.

7. Remove from the oven and let the cookies cool completely on the baking sheet. Cookies can be stored at room temperature or in the refrigerator.

**PREP TIME:** 30 minutes, plus at least 20 minutes chilling time
**COOK TIME:** 17 minutes
**YIELDS:** 18 cookies

### FOR THE CHEESECAKE

8 ounces (1 brick) cream cheese, softened

¾ cup confectioners' sugar

⅛ teaspoon salt

1 teaspoon vanilla extract

### FOR THE COOKIES

1 cup (2 sticks) unsalted butter, softened

1 cup granulated sugar

1 cup firmly packed light brown sugar

2 large eggs

1 teaspoon vanilla extract

2½ cups all-purpose flour

1 teaspoon baking powder

½ teaspoon baking soda

1 teaspoon salt

½ cup dark chocolate chips

½ cup chopped dried cranberries

½ cup chopped walnuts

# Big Island Cookies

*Kick up the usual white chocolate macadamia nut cookie with the sweet tanginess of pineapple and ginger. My Willie Wonka side shines through in this one. The sweet, warming combination evokes the flavors of Hawaii and fills your imagination with visions of paradise. No flight required.*

PREP TIME: 10 minutes
COOK TIME: 15 minutes
YIELDS: 2 dozen cookies

½ cup (2 ounces) dried pineapple

½ cup (2 ounces) candied ginger

½ cup dried coconut flakes

1 tablespoon water

1 cup (2 sticks) unsalted butter, softened

1 cup granulated sugar

½ cup firmly packed light brown sugar

2 large eggs

1 teaspoon vanilla extract

2½ cups all-purpose flour

1 teaspoon baking powder

½ teaspoon baking soda

1 teaspoon salt

1 cup white chocolate chips

½ cup macadamia nuts

1. Preheat the oven to 375 degrees Fahrenheit. Line two baking sheets with parchment paper.

2. In the bowl of a food processor fitted with a blade, combine the pineapple, ginger, coconut flakes, and water. Blend until roughly chopped.

3. In the bowl of a stand mixer fitted with a paddle attachment, cream together the butter, granulated sugar, and brown sugar until light and fluffy, about 2 minutes.

4. Add the eggs one at a time, mixing well after each addition, then mix in the vanilla.

5. In a separate bowl whisk together the flour, baking powder, baking soda, and salt. Gradually add the dry ingredients to the wet ingredients, mixing until just combined.

6. Stir in the fruit mixture, chocolate chips, and nuts.

7. Scoop the dough into 24 domes using a ¼ measuring cup or ice cream scoop.

8. Bake for 12 to 15 minutes, or until the edges are golden brown. The centers may still appear slightly undercooked, but they will firm up as they cool.

9. Remove from the oven and let the cookies cool on the baking sheet for 5 minutes, then transfer them to a wire rack to cool completely.

# Chocolate-Dipped Marshmallow Cookie

*My mom kept a supply of chocolate and marshmallows on hand all year long. They were great in s'mores or Mississippi Mud Pie, but I love them even more when they're in cookie form. These cocoa-infused cookies are topped with marshmallows (go for the best quality you can find), then dipped in milk chocolate. Simple, perfect, and ready to grab for a quick treat whenever the craving hits.*

1. In the bowl of a stand mixer fitted with a paddle attachment, cream together the butter, granulated sugar, and brown sugar until light and fluffy, about 2 minutes, then add the vanilla and mix another 30 seconds.

2. In a separate bowl whisk together the flour, cocoa powder, baking soda, and salt. Gradually add the dry ingredients to the wet ingredients, mixing until just combined. Add the milk and mix 1 minute more.

3. Divide the dough into halves, then shape the dough into thick logs, about 2 inches in diameter. Wrap tightly in plastic wrap and refrigerate for at least 1 hour.

4. Preheat the oven to 350 degrees Fahrenheit. Line 2 baking sheets with parchment paper.

5. Remove the dough from the plastic wrap and cut each log into 12 equal round slices. Bake for 10 minutes, until firm. Remove from the oven and allow to sit until cool enough to handle.

6. In a microwave-safe bowl, melt the chocolate in the microwave in 30-second intervals, stirring between each interval, until melted and smooth.

7. Dip one flat side of a marshmallow into the chocolate, then place the dipped side of the marshmallow on a cookie, and repeat. Allow to set for 15 minutes to adhere to the cookie.

8. Rewarm chocolate and dip each marshmallow cookie halfway into the melted chocolate so that half of each cookie and the marshmallow are covered. Remove to a wire rack to set, or chill in the refrigerator to set more quickly.

**PREP TIME:** 20 minutes, plus setting time
**COOK TIME:** 10 minutes
**YIELDS:** 2 dozen cookies

½ cup (1 stick) unsalted butter, softened

½ cup granulated sugar

½ cup firmly packed dark brown sugar

1 teaspoon vanilla extract

1 cup all-purpose flour

¾ cup unsweetened cocoa powder

½ teaspoon baking soda

¼ teaspoon salt

¼ cup milk

2 cups milk chocolate chips

24 large marshmallows (shown here), or extra-large (2-inch) marshmallows, if preferred

*Tip: These are also great with homemade marshmallows.*

# Chocolate Pistachio Biscotti

*The first location of my chocolate factory was in a historic neighborhood in Memphis, where my business neighbor was an Italian chef who ran a deli. I would stop in and say hello pretty much every morning. He was always working on a fresh batch of biscotti, and I was more than willing to sample a piece. He's the reason I'm such a fan of these little pastries that are a perfect match with my favorite coffee drink, a cortado.*

PREP TIME: 20 minutes, plus setting time
COOK TIME: 40 minutes
YIELDS: 20 pieces

½ cup (1 stick) unsalted butter, room temperature

1 cup granulated sugar

2 large eggs

1 teaspoon vanilla extract

2 cups all-purpose flour

1 teaspoon baking powder

½ teaspoon salt

1 cup shelled pistachios, roughly chopped

1 cup semisweet chocolate chips

1. Preheat the oven to 350 degrees Fahrenheit. Line a baking sheet with parchment paper.

2. In a large mixing bowl beat the butter and sugar together until light and fluffy. Add the eggs and vanilla and beat until well combined.

3. In a separate mixing bowl, whisk together the flour, baking powder, and salt.

4. Gradually add the dry ingredients to the wet ingredients, mixing until a dough forms.

5. Stir in the chopped pistachios until evenly distributed.

6. Turn the dough out onto a lightly floured surface and shape it into two logs, each about 12 inches long and 2 inches wide.

7. Place the logs onto the prepared baking sheet, leaving about 2 inches of space between them.

8. Bake the logs for 25 to 30 minutes, or until they are firm to the touch and slightly cracked on top.

9. Remove the logs from the oven and let them cool on the baking sheet for 10 minutes.

10. Using a sharp knife, cut the logs into ½-inch-thick slices. Arrange the slices on the baking sheet and bake for an additional 10 to 12 minutes, or until they are crispy and dry. Remove the biscotti from the oven and let them cool completely on a wire rack.

11. In a medium microwave-safe mixing bowl, melt the chocolate chips in a microwave in 30-second bursts, or gently over a double boiler, until melted and smooth. Dip the end of each biscotti in the melted chocolate, then place on parchment paper to set, at least 20 minutes, before serving.

# CHAPTER 5

# Fried, Flamed, Baked to Perfection

I grew up loving desserts, such as pineapple upside-down cake, banana pudding, pecan pie, and sweet potato pie. At some point throughout the year, these were in my house, and they always marked special occasions. As I grew up and started baking, I began to play around with the recipes for these childhood favorites. I didn't know it then, but when I was swapping out flavors and building on classics, I was training myself for my future career as a chocolatier.

As you go through these recipes, I highly encourage you to play around with them. Try them first as they are. Then add flavors you love and create your own recipes—they may become beloved family classics. Just remember, if you're not having fun in the kitchen, what's the point of baking at all?

# Fried Chocolate Hand Pies

*My dad taught and coached basketball at my school all through my high school years. Coming home from practice together on Fridays, we would always stop at a gas station in Millington, Tennessee, that sold the best fried chocolate pies. This recipe is my nod to those special days and delicious memories.*

**PREP TIME:** 20 minutes, plus at least 30 minutes chilling time
**COOK TIME:** 20 minutes
**YIELDS:** 8 pies

2 cups all-purpose flour

½ cup unsweetened cocoa powder

½ teaspoon salt

½ cup (1 stick) unsalted butter, chilled and cut into small pieces

⅔ cup cold water

1 cup pecans

1 cup chocolate chips

¼ cup heavy cream

¼ cup granulated sugar

1 teaspoon vanilla extract

1 pinch of smoked flake salt

1 egg, beaten

Neutral cooking oil, for frying

Powdered sugar, for garnish, optional

1. In a large bowl, mix together the flour, cocoa powder, and salt. Cut in the butter until the mixture resembles coarse crumbs.

2. Add the cold water, a little at a time, and mix until the dough comes together.

3. Divide the dough into 8 equal portions and shape into discs. Wrap in plastic wrap and refrigerate for at least 30 minutes.

4. Preheat the oven to 375 degrees Fahrenheit.

5. Toast the pecans until browned, about 6 to 8 minutes. Watch them closely so they don't burn.

6. In a small saucepan combine the chocolate chips, heavy cream, sugar, vanilla, and smoked salt. Cook over low heat, stirring constantly, until the chocolate is melted and the mixture is smooth. Remove from the heat and let cool slightly. Chop the pecans and stir them into the mixture.

7. On a floured surface, roll out each disc of dough into a circle about 6 inches in diameter.

8. Spoon about 2 tablespoons of the chocolate filling onto one half of the circle, leaving a little space around the edges.

9. Brush the edges of the dough with beaten egg and fold the other half of the dough over the filling. Press the edges together to seal. Use a fork to crimp the edges.

10. Fill a heavy-bottomed skillet halfway with cooking oil, and heat to 365 degrees Fahrenheit. Fry the pies in batches until golden and bubbly, about 2 minutes per side. Remove to paper towels to drain and cool slightly. Serve warm, and sprinkle with powdered sugar, if using.

# Chocolate Banana Pudding Torte

*If my family is eating banana pudding, that means it's a special occasion. It's our tradition to reserve that most comforting of comfort desserts for holidays and birthdays, especially since it's a longtime favorite of my dad's. This version, definitely an upscale take on classic Southern banana pudding, is perfect for any holiday or Sunday supper.*

## PREPARE THE CRUST

1. Preheat the oven to 350 degrees Fahrenheit.

2. Using a food processor fitted with a blade, grind the cookies into crumbs. Transfer the cookie crumbs into a medium mixing bowl, and combine with the melted butter and sugar, just until moistened. Press the mixture into a 10-inch tart pan, using the bottom of a glass or mixing cup to even out the crust. Press down very firmly or the crust will fall apart later.

3. Bake for 10 minutes, until lightly golden.

## PREPARE THE TORTE

1. While the crust is baking, prepare the pudding. In a medium saucepan, whisk together the sugar, flour, salt, and cornstarch. In a separate bowl, whisk together the egg yolks and milk. Slowly pour the milk mixture into the saucepan, whisking constantly.

2. Place the saucepan over medium heat and cook, stirring constantly, until the mixture thickens and comes to a boil. Remove from the heat and stir in the vanilla. Transfer to a bowl and cover the pudding by putting plastic wrap directly on the top of the pudding to prevent a skin forming. Chill the pudding for about 30 minutes.

3. Transfer the cooled pudding to the prepared crust, then top with the banana slices.

4. Prepare the ganache. In a small saucepan over medium-low heat, combine the chocolate chips and cream. Heat slowly, stirring often, until chocolate is completely melted and the mixture is smooth and glossy, about 3 to 4 minutes.

5. Pour the ganache over the banana pudding and smooth with a rubber spatula for even coverage. Refrigerate for at least 4 hours to allow the flavors to meld together, until ready to serve.

PREP TIME: 20 minutes, plus at least 4 hours chilling time
COOK TIME: 20 minutes
SERVES: 10

### FOR THE CRUST

1 (11 ounce) box Nilla Wafers

½ cup (1 stick) unsalted butter, melted

¼ cup granulated sugar

### FOR THE TORTE

⅔ cup granulated sugar

¼ cup all-purpose flour

¼ teaspoon salt

1 tablespoon cornstarch

4 large egg yolks

2 cups milk

1 teaspoon vanilla extract

2 ripe bananas, sliced into medallions

1½ cups dark chocolate chips

⅓ cup heavy cream

# Friendsgiving Chocolate Pecan Pie

*The yard at Jean's house was filled with pecan trees, and as long as I can remember, it was my and my younger brother's job to pick them up and bring them inside. To an eight-year-old kid, the trees were massive, and the pecans that fell to the ground were endless. Jean would regularly give people in the neighborhood grocery sacks filled with them because there were so many. From coffee table bowls filled for snacking to countless pies being baked, pecans were a staple you could always expect to be available.*

*This pie—with a sweet molasses filling and roasted pecans, laced with rich chocolate—is a riff on a Southern holiday classic. It's perfect for a family gathering or "Friendsgiving" to show everyone you understood the assignment.*

PREP TIME: 15 minutes
COOK TIME: 65 minutes
SERVES: 10

1½ cups pecan halves

1 pie crust (see page 236)

1 cup semisweet chocolate chips

1 cup dark corn syrup

3 tablespoons unsalted butter

3 large eggs

½ cup granulated sugar

1 teaspoon vanilla extract

¼ teaspoon salt

Whipped cream, optional, for serving

Rum Butter Caramel, optional, for serving (see page 227)

1. Preheat the oven to 350 degrees Fahrenheit.

2. Spread the pecans on a baking sheet lined with parchment paper. Bake for 5 to 10 minutes, until nuts are deep brown and fragrant, but keep an eye on them so they don't burn. Remove from the oven to cool.

3. Unroll the pie crust and place it in a 9-inch pie dish. Trim and crimp the edges as desired.

4. In a small saucepan melt the chocolate chips, corn syrup, and butter over low heat, stirring constantly until smooth. Remove from heat and let cool slightly.

5. In a large mixing bowl whisk together the eggs, sugar, vanilla, and salt until well combined. Stir in the melted chocolate mixture, then fold in the pecans.

6. Pour the filling into the prepared pie crust. Bake for 50 to 55 minutes, or until the center of the pie is set and a toothpick inserted in the center comes out clean.

7. Let the pie cool completely on a wire rack before serving.

8. If using, top each slice with whipped cream drizzled with rum butter caramel before serving.

# Chocolate Pineapple Upside-Down Cake with Grand Marnier–Brown Butter Caramel

*My love for pineapple upside-down cake inspired the Brother Truitt bonbon in the Phillip Ashley Signature Collection. That chocolate—made with Grand Marnier orange liqueur and pineapple—inspired this confection, which turns traditional pineapple upside-down cake on its head. I love this whole cake, but I especially love the caramelization on the pineapple. My mom never liked cooked fruit much, but she would eat this caramelly chocolate version because it's just that good.*

## PREPARE THE PINEAPPLE TOPPING

1. In a small saucepan over medium heat, melt the butter and brown sugar, stirring until sugar is completely dissolved.

2. Transfer the mixture to a 10-inch round nonstick cake pan, then arrange the pineapple slices on top of the caramel. Place a maraschino cherry in the center of each pineapple ring, if using, and set aside.

## PREPARE THE CAKE

1. Preheat the oven to 350 degrees Fahrenheit.

2. In a medium bowl whisk together the flour, cocoa powder, baking powder, baking soda, and salt.

3. In the bowl of a stand mixer fitted with a paddle attachment, cream the butter and granulated sugar until light and fluffy, about 2 minutes.

4. Add the eggs, one at a time, beating well after each, then add the vanilla.

5. Gradually add the dry ingredients to the wet ingredients, alternating with the sour cream and milk, starting and ending with the dry mixture. Mix until just combined.

6. Pour the chocolate cake batter over the pineapple slices and smooth the top.

7. Bake for 40 to 45 minutes, or until a toothpick inserted into the center of the cake comes out clean.

**PREP TIME:** 30 minutes
**COOK TIME:** 45 minutes
**SERVES:** 8 to 10

### FOR THE PINEAPPLE TOPPING

½ cup (1 stick) unsalted butter

1 cup firmly packed light brown sugar

1 (20 ounce) can pineapple slices, drained

Maraschino cherries, optional

### FOR THE CAKE

1¾ cups all-purpose flour

½ cup unsweetened cocoa powder

1½ teaspoons baking powder

½ teaspoon baking soda

¼ teaspoon salt

½ cup (1 stick) unsalted butter, softened

1 cup granulated sugar

2 large eggs

1 teaspoon pure vanilla extract

½ cup sour cream

½ cup whole milk

## FOR THE GRAND MARNIER CARAMEL

1 cup granulated sugar

1/4 cup heavy whipping cream

1/4 cup Grand Marnier, or other orange liqueur

Vanilla ice cream, optional

## MAKE THE GRAND MARNIER CARAMEL

1. While the cake is baking, in a small saucepan heat the granulated sugar over medium-high heat, without stirring, until the sugar begins to turn a golden color. Be patient, as this can take a few minutes. Watch the caramel very carefully. It can go from golden to scorched in the blink of an eye.

2. Once the caramel is a deep golden brown, reduce heat to low. Slowly add the heavy cream, stirring to incorporate. Then add the Grand Marnier, stirring to incorporate. Leave on the heat for another 30 seconds to allow the caramel and liqueur to fully combine. This will also cook out most of the alcohol content but leave the desired orange liqueur flavor behind. Be cautious, as the caramel may bubble up. Remove from the heat and allow to cool slightly.

## ASSEMBLE THE CAKE

1. When the cake is done, remove it from the oven and let it cool in the pan for about 10 minutes.

2. Invert the cake onto a serving platter while it's still warm. Slowly remove the cake pan, allowing the caramel in the pan to drizzle over the cake.

3. Serve cake slices topped with the Grand Marnier caramel and, for an even more indulgent dessert, a scoop of vanilla ice cream.

# Blackout Chocolate Cake

*There are people who like chocolate, and then there are people who can't get enough of the stuff. For them, every chocolate dessert could be richer, darker, and even more full of chocolatey goodness. This cake is for those people. This dense, fudgy cake has the richest chocolate frosting you could imagine and is coated in chocolate shavings because, well, when it comes to the dark stuff, more is definitely more.*

## PREPARE THE CAKE

1. Preheat the oven to 350 degrees Fahrenheit. Grease three 8-inch round cake pans, then line the bottoms with parchment paper.

2. In a medium mixing bowl combine the flour, granulated sugar, brown sugar, cocoa powder, baking soda, baking powder, salt, and espresso powder. Set aside.

3. In the bowl of a stand mixer fitted with a paddle attachment, combine the buttermilk, oil, eggs, and vanilla, and mix 1 minute to combine.

4. Add half the dry mixture, mixing until incorporated, followed by the warm water and then the remaining dry mixture.

5. Bake for about 30 to 34 minutes, until a toothpick comes out clean. Remove from the oven and allow to cool in the pans until cool enough to handle, then remove to a wire rack to finish cooling.

**PREP TIME:** 30 minutes
**COOK TIME:** 40 minutes
**SERVES:** 8 to 10

## FOR THE CAKE

3 cups all-purpose flour

2½ cups granulated sugar

1 cup firmly packed dark brown sugar

1½ cups unsweetened cocoa powder

1 tablespoon baking soda

1½ teaspoons baking powder

1½ teaspoons salt

1 tablespoon plus 1 teaspoon espresso powder

1½ cups buttermilk

1 cup vegetable oil

3 large eggs

1½ tablespoons vanilla extract

1½ cups warm water

## PREPARE THE CHOCOLATE BUTTERCREAM

1. In the bowl of a stand mixer fitted with a wire whisk, cream the butter, confectioners' sugar, cocoa powder, espresso powder, and salt on medium until light and fluffy, about 2 minutes. Add the vanilla, then slowly add the heavy cream until the frosting reaches a spreadable consistency.

2. Generously frost each layer of the cake, stacking as you go.

3. Frost the outside and use any remaining buttercream to create a decorative pattern on top, if you'd like.

4. Press the chocolate shavings into the sides of the cake. Serve.

## FOR THE CHOCOLATE BUTTERCREAM

2 cups bourbon-washed butter (see page 237), or 2 cups (4 sticks) unsalted butter, softened

6 cups confectioners' sugar

1 cup unsweetened cocoa powder

1 teaspoon espresso powder

¼ teaspoon salt

1 tablespoon vanilla bean paste

4 to 6 tablespoons heavy cream or milk

2 to 4 ounces high-quality dark chocolate bars, shaved into curls

# Chocolate Basque Cheesecake

*Cheesecake was one of the first things I taught myself to make. I then began playing with variations as I continued to explore and experiment with flavors. I would bring them to the office of my corporate job for my colleagues to taste. Every version was a hit! This version is a Basque cheesecake: a light and airy crustless cheesecake that originated in Spain's Basque Country. A creamier, custardy version, this type of cheesecake has become an increasingly popular trend in recent years. Here it is enhanced with the decadence of both dark and milk chocolate.*

1. Preheat the oven to 400 degrees Fahrenheit. Grease a 9-inch springform pan with butter or cooking spray, and line the bottom with parchment paper. To get the right fit, trace the circumference of the bottom of the cake pan, then cut the circle out of the paper.

2. In a large mixing bowl beat the cream cheese and sugar until smooth and creamy.

3. Add the eggs one at a time, mixing well after each addition. Mix in the vanilla.

4. In a separate bowl sift together the flour, cocoa powder, and salt.

5. Gradually add the cocoa mixture to the cream cheese mixture, mixing until just combined.

6. Gently stir in the chocolate chips to evenly distribute throughout the batter.

7. Pour the batter into the prepared springform pan, and smooth the top with a spatula.

8. Bake the cheesecake for 45 to 50 minutes, or until the top is set and dark brown.

9. Remove the cheesecake from the oven and let it cool to room temperature.

10. Refrigerate the cheesecake for at least 2 hours. Serve chilled.

PREP TIME: 10 minutes
COOK TIME: 50 minutes
SERVES: 8 to 10

2 cups cream cheese, softened

1¼ cups granulated sugar

4 large eggs

1 tablespoon vanilla extract

½ cup all-purpose flour

½ cup unsweetened cocoa powder

½ teaspoon salt

¼ cup semisweet chocolate chips

¼ cup milk chocolate chips

# Chocolate Barbecue Popcorn

*My barbecue truffle—an ode to the most famous food in my hometown—gets a lot of attention. People just don't expect barbecue flavors in a dessert, but when you think about the molasses, brown sugar, and spices that go into barbecue, it starts to make a lot more sense. This chocolate barbecue popcorn is a standout. Mix up a batch for yourself and another to package as gifts. Once you taste it, you won't want to give yours away.*

PREP TIME: 5 minutes
COOK TIME: 35 minutes
SERVES: 4

¼ cup bacon fat or vegetable oil

½ cup unpopped popcorn kernels

½ cup (1 stick) unsalted butter

2 tablespoons light brown sugar

1½ teaspoons paprika

½ teaspoon chili powder

1½ teaspoons garlic powder

1½ teaspoons onion powder

½ teaspoon salt

½ teaspoon dry mustard

¼ teaspoon cayenne pepper, or more to taste

¼ cup semisweet chocolate chips

1. Preheat oven to 250 degrees Fahrenheit. Line 2 baking sheets with parchment paper.

2. In a large pot with a lid, melt the bacon fat over medium-high heat. Add popcorn kernels.

3. Cook over medium-high heat, shaking often, until the popping of the kernels has slowed, no more than 5 minutes. Make sure not to burn your popcorn.

4. In a small saucepan over medium heat, melt the butter, then add the brown sugar, paprika, chili powder, garlic powder, onion powder, salt, dry mustard, and cayenne, whisking well to combine. Add the chocolate chips and stir until melted. Remove from the heat and drizzle over the popcorn, tossing well to coat evenly.

5. Spread the popcorn over the baking sheets, and bake for about 30 minutes, stirring twice, until the popcorn is dry. Store in an airtight container—if there's any left to store.

# Chocolate Sweet Potato Pie with Brown Sugar Meringue

*The very first chocolate that I created for my signature collection was a sweet potato bonbon named for my grandmother, Jean. Sweet potatoes were plentiful in her house, so there was always a sweet potato pie or casserole around. Here's a recipe for a delightfully chocolate version of Jean's sweet potato pie made even more irresistible with the addition of brown sugar meringue. Although you can brown a meringue in the broiler, I recommend you get a kitchen torch for this recipe. Once you get one, you won't regret having it handy to elevate everyday desserts into caramelized dazzlers.*

## PREPARE THE PIE

1. Preheat the oven to 425 degrees Fahrenheit. Pierce the skin of the sweet potatoes with a fork several times, then place them on a baking sheet lined with foil or parchment paper. Bake for about 45 minutes, until the skin is puffed up and the natural sugar is caramelized.

2. Once cooled, peel off the skin and mash the sweet potatoes, discarding any stringy bits. This can be done up to a day ahead.

3. Reduce the oven temperature to 350 degrees Fahrenheit. Unroll the pie crust and place it in a 9-inch pie dish. Trim and crimp the edges as desired.

4. In a small saucepan melt the chocolate chips and butter over low heat, stirring constantly until smooth. Remove from heat and let cool slightly.

5. In a large mixing bowl combine the sweet potatoes, sugar, melted chocolate mixture, eggs, milk, vanilla, cinnamon, nutmeg, and salt. Mix until smooth.

6. Pour the mixture into the pie crust. Make an egg wash by combining the egg and water in a small bowl, then brushing the mixture on the exposed edges of the pie crust with a pastry brush.

7. Bake the pie for 45 to 50 minutes, or until the filling is set and a toothpick inserted in the center comes out clean.

8. While the pie cools slightly, prepare the meringue. It needs to be added to the pie while the pie is still fairly warm from the oven.

---

PREP TIME: 25 minutes
COOK TIME: 95 minutes
SERVES: 8 to 10

---

FOR THE PIE

2 medium sweet potatoes, mashed (2 cups)

1 pie crust (see page 236)

½ cup semisweet chocolate chips

¼ cup (½ stick) unsalted butter

½ cup granulated sugar

2 large eggs

½ cup milk

1 teaspoon vanilla extract

½ teaspoon ground cinnamon

¼ teaspoon ground nutmeg

⅛ teaspoon salt

1 egg, beaten

1 tablespoon water

## FOR THE BROWN SUGAR MERINGUE

6 large egg whites, room temperature

½ cup firmly packed light brown sugar

¼ teaspoon cream of tartar

2 teaspoons vanilla extract

## PREPARE MERINGUE

1. Place the egg whites, brown sugar, and cream of tartar in the top of a double boiler. Heat over 2 inches of simmering water, whisking constantly until the sugar is dissolved, and the mixture reaches 160 degrees Fahrenheit on an instant-read thermometer. Remove from heat and whisk in the vanilla.

2. Transfer the mixture to the bowl of a stand mixer fitted with a whisk. Beat on high until stiff peaks form, about 5 minutes. Spread the meringue over the pie, making a decorative pattern with the back of a large spoon.

3. Using a kitchen torch, toast the meringue until golden brown. (You can also broil your meringue in the broiler. Preheat the oven to broil with a rack close to the heating element. Once hot, place the pie in the oven for 3 to 5 minutes, until browned.)

4. Serve immediately. Store for 1 day at room temperature or in the refrigerator for up to 5 days.

# Black Velvet Cake with Tanghulu "Glass" Strawberries

*Red velvet cake is a Southern staple, but as you've probably guessed by now, I think everything is better when it is a little bit fancier and includes more chocolate. This variation on red velvet adds chocolate to the cake itself but still has that classic red incorporated from the addition of ruby chocolate to the cream cheese frosting and the topper of gorgeous "glass" candied strawberries, called* tanghulu *in China, where the trend originated. This is admittedly a little over the top. I encourage you to try making the glass strawberries. It is easier than it seems (see page 231). But if they seem like too much, just top the cake with fresh strawberries.*

## PREPARE THE CAKE

1. Preheat the oven to 350 degrees Fahrenheit. Grease three 8-inch round cake pans, then line the bottom of each with parchment paper. To get the right fit, trace the circumference of the bottom of the cake pan, then cut the circle out of the paper.

2. In the bowl of a stand mixer fitted with a paddle attachment, combine the vegetable oil, buttermilk, eggs, vinegar, and vanilla. Mix until combined, about 1 minute. Add the flour, cocoa powder, sugar, baking soda, and salt. Beat on medium for 2 minutes, until smooth.

3. Divide the batter evenly between the pans, then tap them on the counter a few times to remove bubbles from the batter. Bake until a knife inserted in the center of each cake comes out clean, about 28 minutes.

4. Remove from the oven and let cool briefly in the pans, then turn out onto a wire rack to cool completely. Using a wire cake cutter or long knife, trim the rounded top of each cake to a flat surface, then cut each cake horizontally so you have 6 equal layers. Let cool.

PREP TIME: 40 minutes
COOK TIME: 30 minutes
SERVES: 8 to 10

## FOR THE CAKE

1 cup vegetable oil

1½ cups buttermilk

4 large eggs

1½ teaspoons white vinegar

1½ teaspoons vanilla extract

3½ cups all-purpose flour

1 cup black cocoa powder

2 cups granulated sugar

1½ teaspoons baking soda

1½ teaspoons salt

## PREPARE THE FROSTING

1.  In the mixing bowl of a stand mixer fitted with a balloon whip, combine the cream cheese and butter. Mix on high speed until creamy, about 1 minute.

2.  Add the sugar, vanilla, and salt. Mix on low to combine, then increase speed to high and mix for 2 minutes, until whipped and smooth.

3.  Generously frost the top of each layer of the cake, stacking as you go. For the final layer, invert the cut side so the smooth side is on top. (This will prevent crumbs from getting into the top frosting.)

4.  Once all 6 layers are stacked, insert a straw or cake dowel vertically in the center of the cake to keep the layers from sliding. Frost the sides and top, and use any remaining buttercream to create a decorative pattern on top, if you'd like.

5.  Arrange the strawberries on top in the center of the cake, or any way you think they look nice. Add ruby shavings to the bottom of the cake. Refrigerate until ready to serve.

### FOR THE CREAM CHEESE FROSTING

24 ounces (3 bricks) cream cheese, softened

1½ cups (3 sticks) unsalted butter, softened

6 cups confectioners' sugar

2 teaspoons pure vanilla extract, or vanilla bean paste

½ teaspoon salt

### TO ASSEMBLE THE CAKE

1 (3.1 ounce) bar ruby chocolate, shaved

6 to 8 tanghulu "glass" strawberries (see page 231)

---

*Tip: To make chocolate shavings, use a vegetable peeler along the edge of a chocolate bar that's either been chilled or room temperature. Try not to handle them and simply let them freely fall into a dish, and then set aside until ready to use.*

# Brûléed Chocolate Cupcakes

*I love a variety of textures in desserts. Some of my friends can't handle that much variety because they aren't "texture people"—as they often remind me. I have a lot of fun getting them to tiptoe outside of their comfort zone! These cupcakes have three gorgeous textures: dense chocolate cake that's almost like a brownie, silky vanilla bean pudding, and a crisp sugar top—the hallmark of a great creme brûlée.*

## PREPARE THE FILLING

1. In a small bowl dissolve the cornstarch in two tablespoons of the milk. Whisk in the egg yolks and set aside.

2. In a medium saucepan over medium heat, combine the cream, remaining milk, sugar, and salt. Split open the vanilla bean lengthwise using a sharp knife and scrape out the seeds. Put the seeds and bean pod into the pan. Heat until hot but not boiling, about 5 minutes, then remove the bean pod.

3. Whisk in the cornstarch mixture, and cook about 5 minutes more, stirring constantly, until the pudding is thickened and just coming to a boil. Remove from the heat and stir in the butter until fully incorporated. Transfer to a bowl, then cover with plastic wrap directly on top of the pudding. Refrigerate for at least 1 hour.

**PREP TIME:** 30 minutes, plus at least 1 hour chilling time
**COOK TIME:** 35 minutes
**YIELDS:** 12 cupcakes

## FOR THE FILLING

1½ tablespoons cornstarch

½ cup whole milk, divided

1 egg yolk

¾ cup heavy cream

⅓ cup granulated sugar

Pinch of salt

1 vanilla bean, or ½ teaspoon vanilla bean paste

1 tablespoon unsalted butter, softened

## FOR THE CUPCAKES

6 ounces bittersweet chocolate, chopped

3/4 cup (1½ sticks) unsalted butter, plus more for greasing

1 cup granulated sugar

1 teaspoon vanilla extract

3 large eggs

1 cup all-purpose flour

½ teaspoon salt

½ cup turbinado sugar

---

*Option: If you'd like to add extra flair, top with chocolate buttercream or carry the custard all the way across and brûlée the entire top.*

## PREPARE THE CUPCAKES

1.  Preheat the oven to 325 degrees Fahrenheit. Grease a 12-piece cupcake pan.

2.  In a small saucepan melt the chopped chocolate and butter over low heat, stirring constantly until smooth. Remove from the heat and immediately stir in the granulated sugar so it dissolves completely.

3.  Add the vanilla and eggs, mixing well. Stir in the flour and salt.

4.  Transfer the batter to the cupcake wells, filling each nearly to the top. These won't rise, so you want them to be as tall as they can be before they go into the oven.

5.  Bake for 20 to 22 minutes until baked through and a knife comes out almost completely clean. (If you wait until a knife comes out completely clean, they'll be overcooked.) Remove the pan from the oven and let cool about 10 minutes, then turn the cupcakes out onto a wire rack to cool completely.

6.  Assemble the cupcakes just before you're ready to serve them. Using a small kitchen knife, carve out the center of the cupcakes, leaving a conical hole about 1½ inches in diameter at the top. Be careful not to pierce through the bottom. Fill each cupcake with pudding just to the top but not over.

7.  Sprinkle the turbinado sugar over the cupcake tops, covering the pudding, dividing evenly between the cakes. Using a kitchen torch, carefully brown the sugar, avoiding touching the cake with the flame. Let sit a few minutes before serving.

# CHAPTER 6

# A Spoonful of Chocolate

Going to the same school where my dad was a teacher meant he was also my transportation. During my elementary school years, he would often play show tunes during the ride. "A Spoonful of Sugar" from *Mary Poppins* not only inspired the name of this chapter but, with the help of other songs like it, fueled the imagination that would rocket my recipes into the creative stratosphere. Those drives with my dad were where I first began to dream up fantastical creations like the ones you will explore in this chapter.

The common thread here is chocolate you eat with a spoon: puddings, ice creams, gelatos, and soufflés. Chocolate is incredibly versatile. It can be used to make treats that break with a satisfying snap, and it can be used to make decadent, pillowy desserts that are spooned into bowls. Chocolate makes everything better.

# Sweet Potato Sticky Toffee Pudding

*My grandmother grew sweet potatoes, and she used them in just about everything. As an adult, I have spent a great deal of time learning about the varieties of sweet potato that exist, from the one most know and love (which is actually called the "Beauregard"—I just love that name) to the distant cousin, yuca. My variation on the classic British sticky toffee pudding celebrates the flavors of my favorite Southern holiday desserts, made even better with chocolate and salted caramel. This dessert is perfect for the autumn or winter, but truthfully, there's no bad time to indulge.*

## PREPARE THE PUDDING

1. Preheat the oven to 425 degrees Fahrenheit. Pierce the skin of the sweet potatoes with a fork several times, then place them on a baking sheet lined with foil or parchment paper. Bake for about 45 minutes, until the skin is puffed up and the natural sugar is caramelized.

2. Once cooled, peel off the skin and mash the sweet potatoes in a bowl, discarding any stringy bits. Stir in the cinnamon and nutmeg.

3. Lower the oven to 350 degrees Fahrenheit.

4. In a medium saucepan combine the dates and water. Bring to a boil, then reduce the heat to medium and let it simmer until the dates are soft, about 5 minutes. Remove from heat.

5. In the bowl of a stand mixer fitted with a paddle attachment, cream together the butter and turbinado sugar until light and fluffy, about 1 minute. Add the eggs and vanilla, mixing until well combined, another minute.

6. In another bowl, combine the flour, cocoa powder, baking powder, and baking soda.

7. Add the dry ingredients to the butter and sugar mixture, alternating with the mashed sweet potatoes. Start and finish with the dry ingredients, mixing until everything is well combined, about 2 minutes.

8. Add the softened date mixture to the batter and mix until just combined.

PREP TIME: 20 minutes
COOK TIME: 90 minutes
SERVES: 12 to 16

### FOR THE PUDDING

2 medium sweet potatoes (2 cups mashed)

1 teaspoon cinnamon

½ teaspoon nutmeg

½ cup pitted dates, finely chopped

1 cup water

½ cup (1 stick) unsalted butter, plus more for greasing

½ cup turbinado (or firmly packed dark brown) sugar

2 eggs

1 teaspoon vanilla bean paste

1¼ cups all-purpose flour

½ cup unsweetened cocoa powder

1 teaspoon baking powder

½ teaspoon baking soda

## FOR THE TOFFEE SAUCE

1 cup turbinado (or firmly packed dark brown) sugar

½ cup heavy cream

½ cup (1 stick) unsalted butter

½ teaspoon vanilla extract

Vanilla ice cream, optional

Whipped cream, optional

9. Pour the batter into a greased 9 x 12-inch baking dish. Bake for about 30 to 35 minutes or until a toothpick inserted into the center comes out clean.

10. While the pudding is baking, make the toffee sauce. In a medium saucepan combine turbinado sugar, heavy cream, and butter. Cook over low heat, stirring until the sugar is dissolved and the mixture is smooth. Simmer for about 5 minutes until it thickens slightly. Remove from heat and stir in the vanilla.

11. Once the pudding is done baking, remove it from the oven and let it cool for a few minutes. Poke holes in the cake and pour the toffee sauce over the whole thing.

12. Serve the pudding warm. You can also serve it with a scoop of vanilla ice cream or a dollop of whipped cream for extra indulgence.

# Mocha Tres Leches Cake

*I am a texture person, in the sense that I love them all! What's better than a cake soaked in sweet cream? The first time I made a tres leches was for a Spanish 2 class project in high school. The assignment was to make a popular Latin American dish as part of our exam. This mocha tres leches is my adaptation of that traditional recipe, sprinkled with about thirty years of experience—and a lifetime of loving chocolate.*

## PREPARE THE CHOCOLATE SPONGE CAKE

1. Preheat the oven to 350 degrees Fahrenheit. Grease and flour an 8 x 10-inch baking dish.

2. In a medium bowl sift together the flour, cocoa powder, baking powder, baking soda, and salt.

3. In a large mixing bowl beat the eggs with an electric mixer on high speed until thick and pale, about 5 minutes.

4. Gradually add the granulated sugar to the eggs, continuing to beat until the mixture is light and fluffy.

5. In a small bowl combine the milk, vegetable oil, and vanilla.

6. With the mixer on low speed, gradually add the dry ingredients to the egg mixture, alternating with the milk mixture. Begin and end with the dry ingredients, mixing just until combined. Do not overmix.

7. Pour the batter into the pan and bake for 35 to 40 minutes, or until a toothpick inserted into the center of the cakes comes out clean.

## PREPARE THE MOCHA MILK MIXTURE

1. In a large measuring cup or bowl, whisk together the evaporated milk, sweetened condensed milk, heavy cream, coffee, and cocoa powder until well combined.

2. Once the cake has cooled, use a fork or skewer to poke holes all over the surface of the cake.

3. Slowly pour the mocha milk mixture over the cake, making sure to cover the entire surface. Let the cake soak for at least 1 hour, preferably overnight, in the refrigerator.

---

**PREP TIME:** 35 minutes, plus soaking overnight
**COOK TIME:** 40 minutes
**SERVES:** 10 to 12

---

### FOR THE CHOCOLATE SPONGE CAKE

1 cup all-purpose flour

¼ cup unsweetened cocoa powder

1 teaspoon baking powder

½ teaspoon baking soda

¼ teaspoon salt

4 large eggs, room temperature

1 cup granulated sugar

½ cup whole milk, room temperature

½ cup vegetable oil

1 teaspoon vanilla extract

### FOR THE MOCHA MILK MIXTURE

1 (12 ounce) can evaporated milk

1 (14 ounce) can sweetened condensed milk

½ cup heavy cream

¼ cup strong brewed coffee, cooled

2 tablespoons unsweetened cocoa powder

## PREPARE THE WHIPPED MOCHA TOPPING

1. In a large bowl whip the heavy cream with the confectioners' sugar, vanilla, and instant coffee granules (if using) until stiff peaks form.

2. Spread the whipped cream evenly over the top of the cake. Garnish with chocolate shavings or a dusting of cocoa powder, if desired. Serve chilled.

### FOR THE WHIPPED MOCHA TOPPING

1 cup heavy cream

¼ cup confectioners' sugar

1 teaspoon vanilla extract

1 teaspoon instant coffee granules, optional

Chocolate shavings or unsweetened cocoa powder for dusting or garnish, optional

# Chocolate Soufflé

*I first fell in love with this classic dessert at Erling Jensen, a fine dining restaurant in Memphis. It's one of those recipes that will impress pretty much anyone, although it is one you don't see on restaurant menus very often anymore. It may take a time or two to master the big rise needed. Once you've mastered it, it's worth having in the repertoire when the occasion calls for you to flex.*

1. Preheat the oven to 375 degrees Fahrenheit. Butter a 10-cup soufflé dish and dust with granulated sugar.

2. In a medium saucepan over medium heat, melt the butter. Whisk in the flour until smooth and cook for about 1 to 2 minutes, stirring constantly.

3. Gradually whisk in the milk until the mixture is smooth. Bring to a simmer and cook until thickened, 1 to 2 minutes.

4. Remove the pan from the heat and add the chopped chocolate. Stir until the chocolate is melted and the mixture is smooth.

5. In a separate bowl whisk together the egg yolks and ¼ cup of the granulated sugar until pale and thick, about 2 minutes.

6. Gradually whisk the chocolate mixture into the egg yolk mixture until combined.

7. In a separate bowl beat the egg whites and cream of tartar until foamy. Gradually add the remaining ¼ cup of the granulated sugar and continue beating until stiff peaks form.

8. Gently fold the egg whites into the chocolate mixture, being careful not to deflate the mixture.

9. Pour the mixture into the prepared soufflé dish and smooth the top with a spatula.

10. Bake for 25 to 30 minutes, or until the soufflé is puffed and set.

11. Dust with powdered sugar and serve immediately.

**PREP TIME:** 10 minutes
**COOK TIME:** 40 minutes
**SERVES:** 6 to 8

¼ cup (½ stick) unsalted butter, plus extra for greasing

¼ cup all-purpose flour

1 cup milk

4 ounces bittersweet chocolate, finely chopped

3 egg yolks

½ cup granulated sugar, divided

4 egg whites

Pinch of cream of tartar

Powdered sugar, for dusting

# Chocolate-Bourbon Pots de Créme with Smoked Sea Salt

*Pot de Créme is chocolate pudding's fancy French cousin. It's denser and more decadent than a fluffy mousse and is typically baked in a bain-marie, otherwise known as a hot water bath. My version delivers all that beloved decadence without needing to turn on your oven. What little work is involved is all on top of the stove. If you want to be a dinner party legend, I highly recommend jazzing it up with a big splash of bourbon and finishing with a sprinkling of smoked flaky sea salt for a touch of sparkle. The salt adds an unexpected layer of complexity that amplifies the oak of the spirit.*

**PREP TIME:** 10 minutes, plus at least 4 hours chilling time, or overnight
**COOK TIME:** 15 minutes
**SERVES:** 6 to 10, depending on the size of your serving dishes

1½ cups heavy cream

¾ cup whole milk

6 large egg yolks

½ cup granulated sugar

¼ teaspoon vanilla extract

2½ cups (15 ounces) semisweet chocolate chips

½ cup bourbon

Smoked, flaked sea salt, for garnish (I like Maldon)

1. In a medium-sized, heavy-bottomed saucepan, heat the cream and milk over medium-low heat just until small bubbles begin to form. Do not let it boil.

2. In a medium mixing bowl whisk together the egg yolks, sugar, and vanilla until fully incorporated.

3. Temper the egg yolk mixture by slowly adding ½ cup of the hot cream in a steady stream to the mixture, whisking to combine.

4. Add the tempered eggs to the hot cream. Reduce the heat to low and cook, whisking constantly, until the custard thickens and coats the back of a wooden spoon.

5. Remove from the heat.

6. Place the chocolate chips in a medium-sized microwave-safe bowl and heat in 30- to 45-second intervals, stirring after each interval to prevent scorching, until completely melted.

7. Stir the melted chocolate into the custard until the mixture is thoroughly combined.

8. Add the bourbon and stir until well combined.

9. Divide evenly into serving dishes such as ramekins, wine glasses, or teacups. Chill for at least 4 hours, or overnight. Sprinkle the pots de créme with a little sea salt before serving.

# Vegan Avocado Chocolate Pudding

*For National Women's History Month, I created a special collection with chocolates matched to the personalities of high-achieving women, which included a tasty dairy-free chocolate with pureed avocado. This plant-based dessert is based on that confection. It might sound unusual to people who are used to desserts full of cream and butter, but trust me, one bite will convince you that this healthier treat doesn't miss them.*

1. In a small saucepan over medium-high heat combine the turbinado sugar and water. Bring to a boil, stirring to dissolve the sugar granules into a simple syrup, about 3 to 4 minutes. Add the chocolate and stir until melted. Remove from the heat and allow to cool completely, about 10 minutes.

2. Transfer the mixture to a food processor fitted with a blade. Remove the inner flesh from the avocados, discarding the pits and skin, and add that to the food processor. Add the cocoa powder, vanilla, and salt. Blend the mixture for 1 minute, until the ingredients meld together. While the processor is going, slowly add the milk until the mixture becomes creamy and glossy. You might not need all of it.

3. Transfer into individual serving dishes and chill for at least 2 hours. When ready to serve, top with fresh berries and plant-based whipped cream, if desired.

**PREP TIME**: 10 minutes, plus at least 2 hours chilling time
**COOK TIME**: 5 minutes
**SERVES**: 4

½ cup turbinado sugar or raw brown sugar

½ cup water

½ cup dark chocolate chunks

2 ripe avocados

¼ cup unsweetened cocoa powder

1 teaspoon vanilla extract

¼ teaspoon salt

2 to 3 tablespoons plant-based milk (I like oat milk)

Berries and plant-based whipped cream, optional

# Key Lime White Chocolate Pudding in Chocolate Bowls

*A key lime dessert is such a refreshing summer treat—or a nice taste of warm weather during the colder months. This sweet, tart dessert is deceptively simple. Chocolate bowls are super easy to make but look like a showstopper, and the pudding comes together in minutes. Keep this one up your sleeve for when you're really trying to impress your guests.*

PREP TIME: 10 minutes, plus at least 2 hours chilling time
COOK TIME: 10 minutes
SERVES: 4

1 cup white chocolate chips

¼ cup cornstarch

¼ cup granulated sugar

¼ teaspoon salt

2½ cups whole milk

4 large egg yolks

¼ cup key lime juice

1 teaspoon vanilla extract

Zest of 1 key lime, divided

4 chocolate bowls (see page 232)

Whipped cream, optional

Key lime slices, for garnish

Crumbled graham crackers, for garnish

1. In a small saucepan over low heat or in 30-second bursts in the microwave, melt the white chocolate chips, stirring constantly until smooth. Remove from heat.

2. In a medium saucepan over medium heat whisk together the cornstarch, sugar, and salt. Gradually whisk in the milk until smooth. Heat until simmering, 2 to 3 minutes.

3. In a separate bowl whisk the egg yolks. Gradually pour the hot milk mixture into the egg yolks, whisking constantly.

4. Return the mixture to the saucepan and cook over medium heat, stirring constantly, until it thickens and comes to a boil, 2 to 3 minutes.

5. Remove the saucepan from the heat and whisk in the melted white chocolate, key lime juice, vanilla, and key lime zest until well combined.

6. Transfer to a mixing bowl and place plastic wrap directly on the surface of the pudding to prevent a skin forming. Refrigerate for at least 2 hours or until set.

7. When ready to serve, portion the pudding equally into the 4 chocolate bowls. Serve garnished with lime slices, and finished with whipped cream and graham cracker crumbles as desired.

# Chocolate Mascarpone Gelato

*When I was growing up, my grandmother was the queen of homemade ice cream. As with many things, my love of ice cream started in her house. I especially love a good gelato, which reminds me of the texture and taste of Jean's creations. This is an easy-to-make recipe, but it does require an ice cream maker. Once you make the investment, you'll be surprised at how simple it is to whip up a fresh batch of whatever flavor you're in the mood for.*

1. In a saucepan heat the milk and cream over medium heat until it begins to steam, but do not let it boil, about 3 to 4 minutes.

2. In a separate bowl whisk the egg yolks until they are light and frothy. Whisk in the sugar and cocoa powder until well combined.

3. Slowly pour the hot milk and cream mixture into the egg mixture, whisking constantly.

4. Pour the mixture back into the saucepan and cook over low heat, stirring constantly, until the mixture thickens enough to coat the back of a spoon, another 5 to 7 minutes. Remove from heat and let the mixture cool.

5. Once the mixture has cooled, whisk in the mascarpone cheese and vanilla until well combined.

6. Pour the mixture into an ice cream maker and churn according to the manufacturer's instructions. Transfer the gelato to a container and freeze until firm, about 2 to 4 hours. Serve alongside a baked dessert, or drizzle it with chocolate sauce to enjoy on its own.

**PREP TIME:** 5 minutes, plus at least 8 hours chilling and freezing time
**COOK TIME:** 12 minutes
**SERVES:** 4 to 6

2 cups whole milk

1 cup heavy cream

4 egg yolks

3/4 cup granulated sugar

1/4 cup unsweetened cocoa powder

1/2 cup mascarpone cheese, softened

1 teaspoon vanilla extract

# Cherry Cordial Gelato

*Here's something you probably won't expect me to say: I don't often eat the chocolates I make every day in my shop. There has to be some sort of control, right? One that I will frequently reach for, though, is our cherry cordial. It's especially funny because I made it as a spoof to try to improve on the cherry cordials we always had around—which I never liked—when I was a kid. This gelato takes the flavors of that chocolate, one of our most popular confections, and turns it into a cool, creamy treat you can enjoy on its own or serve alongside other desserts, like Blackout Chocolate Cake (see page 137) or the Simply Perfect Fudge Brownie (see page 94).*

---

PREP TIME: 5 minutes, plus at least 2 hours chilling time
COOK TIME: 12 minutes
SERVES: 4 to 6

---

2 cups whole milk

1 cup heavy cream

3/4 cup granulated sugar

4 large egg yolks

1/2 cup dark chocolate, chopped into small pieces

2 tablespoons maraschino cherry syrup (from a jar of maraschino cherries)

1/2 cup maraschino cherries, coarsely chopped

1. In a medium saucepan combine the whole milk, heavy cream, and granulated sugar. Heat the mixture over medium heat until it reaches a simmer, stirring occasionally to dissolve the sugar.

2. In a separate bowl whisk the egg yolks until smooth. Temper the eggs by slowly pouring about 1/2 cup of the hot milk mixture into the egg yolks, whisking constantly.

3. Pour the tempered yolks into the saucepan with the remaining milk mixture. Cook over medium heat, stirring constantly, until the mixture thickens and coats the back of a spoon, about 5 to 7 minutes. Do not let it boil.

4. Allow the mixture to cool slightly, then cover and refrigerate for at least 4 hours or overnight.

5. Once the mixture is chilled, pour it into an ice cream maker and churn according to the manufacturer's instructions. This usually takes around 20 to 30 minutes.

6. While the gelato is churning, melt the dark chocolate in bursts in the microwave or over a double boiler until melted and smooth. Let it cool slightly.

7. When the gelato is almost done churning, slowly drizzle the melted chocolate into the ice cream maker. The churning motion will create ribbons of chocolate throughout the gelato.

8. Slowly add the syrup and cherries into the ice cream maker.

9. Transfer the churned gelato into a lidded container, and freeze for at least 4 hours or until firm.

# Baked Memphis

*The classic Baked Alaska is having a serious comeback these days. I wanted to make a version that reflects my hometown. The Baked Memphis was inspired by Memphis's favorite son and is good enough for Elvis himself. A peanut butter brownie base is topped with a banana caramel sauce, ice cream, and brown sugar meringue. It's also another excuse to break out the kitchen torch. Use whatever ice cream you prefer for this one. Chocolate, vanilla, rocky road, or chocolate chip would be great.*

## PREPARE THE BASE

1. Set out the ice cream for 20 minutes to allow it to soften. Line the inside of an 8-inch-diameter mixing bowl with plastic wrap, leaving ample plastic wrap overhanging the sides, then transfer the softened ice cream to the bowl. Press down to eliminate air pockets and smooth the top as best you can, then wrap the overhanging plastic wrap over the top and cover with more plastic wrap. Freeze overnight. (This can be done a couple of days in advance.)

## PREPARE THE BROWNIE

1. Preheat the oven to 350 degrees Fahrenheit. Grease an 8-inch round cake pan.

2. In a small saucepan over medium heat, melt the butter and dark chocolate, stirring until fully incorporated, about 3 to 4 minutes. Remove from the heat and allow to cool slightly.

3. In a large mixing bowl whisk the butter mixture and sugar together. Add the vanilla and eggs, and stir to combine.

4. Add the flour, cocoa powder, and salt, and stir until just mixed. Transfer the mixture to the prepared cake pan.

5. In a small bowl microwave the peanut butter for 20 seconds to soften. Swirl the peanut butter across the top of the batter with a rubber spatula.

6. Bake until a knife inserted into the center of the pan comes out not quite clean but not fully coated in batter, about 25 minutes. Remove from the oven and allow to cool completely.

---

**PREP TIME:** 60 minutes, plus freezing overnight
**COOK TIME:** 60 minutes
**SERVES:** 8 to 10

---

### FOR THE BASE

2 quarts ice cream, flavor of your choice

### FOR THE PEANUT BUTTER BROWNIE

$\frac{1}{2}$ cup (1 stick) unsalted butter, plus more for greasing

$\frac{3}{4}$ cup dark chocolate chips

$\frac{3}{4}$ cup granulated sugar

1 tablespoon vanilla extract

2 large eggs

$\frac{3}{4}$ cup all-purpose flour

$\frac{1}{4}$ cup unsweetened cocoa powder

$\frac{1}{2}$ teaspoon salt

$\frac{1}{3}$ cup peanut butter

## FOR THE BANANA CARAMEL SAUCE

1 tablespoon butter

2 medium ripe bananas, sliced into rounds

2 cups granulated sugar

1 cup heavy cream

1 tablespoon vanilla bean paste

½ teaspoon kosher salt

½ cup light corn syrup

## FOR THE ICE CREAM AND MERINGUE

6 large egg whites

¾ cup granulated sugar

⅛ teaspoon salt

¼ teaspoon cream of tartar

2 teaspoons vanilla extract

## PREPARE THE CARAMEL

1. While the brownie is cooling, prepare the caramel. In a skillet over medium heat, melt the butter. Add the bananas and sauté until soft, about 2 to 3 minutes. Remove from heat.

2. In a heavy-bottomed pot heat the sugar over high heat. Once it has begun melting, gently move the sugar around to prevent scorching. Do this as little as possible—don't fully stir it.

3. When the sugar has the consistency of wet sand, reduce heat to medium. Move sugar around a bit, breaking up any clumps. Once the sugar is about 90 percent melted, turn off the heat and allow the residual heat to finish melting it, about 2 to 3 minutes.

4. While the sugar is cooking, combine the cream, vanilla bean paste, salt, and corn syrup in a small saucepan over medium heat. Warm the mixture until just before boiling and stir well.

5. Slowly pour the cream mixture into the hot caramel. Give the sugar only about 2 to 3 minutes off the heat before doing this or it will burn. Let bubbles settle, then stir with a whisk until well combined. Pour through a strainer to remove any remaining sugar clumps, then stir in the bananas. Allow to cool completely before proceeding.

6. Remove the ice cream from the freezer and uncover the top of the plastic wrap. Pour the caramel over the ice cream, making sure the bananas are evenly distributed, then invert the brownie onto the caramel so the flat bottom is facing up. Rewrap and freeze for 1 hour.

## PREPARE THE MERINGUE

1. While the cake is freezing, prepare the meringue. Place the egg whites, sugar, salt, and cream of tartar in the top of a double boiler. Heat over 2 inches of simmering water, whisking constantly, until the sugar is dissolved, and the mixture reaches 175 degrees Fahrenheit on an instant-read thermometer. Remove from heat and whisk in the vanilla.

2. Transfer the mixture to the bowl of a stand mixer fitted with a whisk. Beat on high until stiff peaks form, about 5 to 8 minutes.

## ASSEMBLE THE CAKE

1. Remove the cake from the freezer and unwrap the plastic covering the brownie section. Invert the cake onto a serving platter and fully discard all plastic wrap. Spread the meringue over the cake, making a decorative pattern with the back of a large spoon. Make sure all the ice cream is completely covered.

2. Using a kitchen torch, toast the meringue until golden brown. Serve immediately. Store any leftovers in the freezer.

# CHAPTER 7

# "Choctails" and Other Sips

**A** big part of my chocolate education has come from talking with people who have mastered the art of flavor. Who better than mixologists and bartenders, the people who mix our amazing cocktails and come up with novel twists to keep flavors fresh? I wanted to transfer that knowledge into chocolates—and, in this chapter, bring it back out of truffles and into cocktails.

Chocolate cocktails get a bad rap. Too often people assume a cocktail that incorporates chocolate can only be a sickly sweet dessert martini. While those are out there, there are also sophisticated libations that utilize chocolate's earthy, rich flavors to amplify similar flavors in spirits. While I'm not above a chocolate martini every once in a while, more often I prefer drinks in the second category. This chapter is full of unexpected takes on classic cocktails, with a few fun, adult versions of nostalgic chocolate treats thrown in for good measure.

Please note that the consumption of alcoholic beverages is only allowed for individuals of legal drinking age. Drink responsibly.

# Mississippi Mud Hot Chocolate

*As a kid, when my family and I visited relatives, I used to run through the thick, rich Mississippi mud while having water fights. This chocolate drink reminds me of those good times (and that reddish-brown mud that took my mom forever to scrub out of my clothes). It is a vast improvement on any of those overly sweet cocoa mixes. This is an adults-only version with a shot of your favorite bourbon. If you are making it for kids, just leave that out.*

1. In a heavy-bottomed pot combine the milk and cream. Scrape the seeds from the vanilla bean into the pot and add the pod. Cook over medium heat until hot, about 3 minutes.

2. Add the dark and milk chocolate. Stir to melt and incorporate. Turn the heat down to low. Add the cinnamon and stir.

3. Remove the vanilla bean pod. Continue to simmer until the mixture thickens. Take care not to scorch.

4. Stir in the bourbon and remove from the heat. Serve in mugs and garnish with marshmallows.

PREP TIME: 10 minutes
SERVES: 2

1½ cups whole milk

½ cup heavy cream

1 vanilla bean, split lengthwise

4 ounces dark chocolate

2 ounces milk chocolate

½ teaspoon cinnamon

2 ounces bourbon

Mini marshmallows, for garnish

# Chocolate Milkshake for Grown-Ups

*When I'm craving something cold and sweet, I'm much more likely to go for a delicious milkshake than a cone of ice cream. With this grown-up version, I wanted to go as over-the-top as possible for those times when I'm in the mood to have some fun. If a fresh s'more isn't your thing, feel free to add a cookie or a strawberry as garnish—or why not go even bigger and add a cupcake, or even a whole slice of something sweet? In my book, you can have your milkshake and eat your cake too.*

PREP TIME: 10 minutes

SERVES: 2

### FOR THE MILKSHAKE

Chocolate syrup, for coating and rimming the glass

Crushed graham crackers, for rimming the glass

3 ounces premium vodka

3 ounces chocolate liqueur

4 cups chocolate ice cream

### FOR THE S'MORES GARNISH

2 sheets graham crackers

2 ounces dark chocolate, divided, from a chocolate bar

Marshmallows

### PREPARE THE MILKSHAKE

1. Pour some chocolate syrup into a saucer or a small, shallow dish. In another saucer or dish place the graham cracker crumbs. Dip the rim of a pint glass in the chocolate syrup, then the crumbs. Repeat for the second glass.

2. Combine the vodka, liqueur, and ice cream in a blender and blend on high until smooth, about 2 minutes.

3. Drizzle some chocolate syrup down the insides of the pint glasses, then immediately fill with the milkshake.

### PREPARE THE S'MORES

1. Break each graham cracker in half to make 4 equal squares. Top 2 pieces with 1 ounce of chocolate each.

2. Spear a marshmallow on a roasting fork, then toast the marshmallow using a kitchen torch until golden and bubbling. Using another graham cracker square, transfer the marshmallow onto the chocolate to make a sandwich.

3. Repeat with the other s'more. Use as garnish on the milkshakes and serve immediately.

# All-Pink-Everything Sparkling Cocktail

*In my mind, champagne and sparkling wine aren't only for special occasions—they make any day a day worth celebrating. This twist on the champagne cocktail takes the classic drink and makes it, well, pink. Sparkling rosé and a chocolate-covered strawberry make this the perfect way to celebrate Valentine's Day, a bachelorette party, or any day that could benefit from a touch of bubbly.*

1. In two champagne flutes, divide the raspberry liqueur and crème de cacao evenly.

2. Fill almost to the top with bubbly.

3. Garnish with raspberries and ruby chocolate, if using, and serve.

**PREP TIME:** 10 minutes, plus setting time
**SERVES:** 2

1 ounce raspberry liqueur (I like Chambord)

1 ounce clear crème de cacao

8 ounces rosé champagne or sparkling rosé, chilled

2 raspberries

Ruby chocolate shavings, optional, for garnish

# Chocolate Memphian Cocktail

*I love a Manhattan, but I love it more when it's an ode to my hometown. This version elevates the whiskey's chocolate notes with chocolate liqueur and bitters. A piece of chocolate on the side doesn't hurt either!*

PREP TIME: 5 minutes

SERVES: 2

4 ounces rye whiskey
(I use Blue Note Honey
Rye, made in Memphis)

1½ ounces sweet vermouth

1 ounce chocolate liqueur

4 dashes bitters (I use
Angostura cocoa bitters)

2 maraschino cherries

1. Chill two martini glasses in the freezer for about 10 minutes.

2. Fill a cocktail shaker with ice, then add the rye whiskey, vermouth, and chocolate liqueur.

3. Add the bitters and gently stir for 10 to 15 seconds, blending ingredients well.

4. Place a maraschino cherry in the bottom of each of two coupe or martini glasses.

5. Place a strainer over the top of the shaker and divide the liquid between the two chilled glasses. Serve immediately.

# Chocolate Espresso Cocktail

*Nothing beats a classic espresso martini, unless—and you probably saw this coming—you add chocolate. My version skips out on the cream, but if you want yours light, just add a dash of heavy cream to the shaker.*

1. Chill two martini glasses in the freezer for about 10 minutes.

2. Fill a cocktail shaker with ice cubes. Add the vodka, coffee liqueur, crème de cacao, and cooled espresso to the shaker.

3. Secure the lid on the shaker and shake vigorously for about 15 to 20 seconds, until the mixture is well-chilled and frothy.

4. Strain the mixture into the chilled martini glasses. Garnish with chocolate shavings, or if you're looking for a more filling treat, add a chocolate-dipped biscotti (see page 124).

**PREP TIME:** 5 minutes
**SERVES:** 2

3 ounces premium vodka

2 ounces coffee liqueur (I use Kahlúa)

2 ounces crème de cacao

2 ounces freshly brewed espresso, cooled

Chocolate shavings, for garnish

# Uncle Nearest Queen V Toddy

*I'm a huge fan of Uncle Nearest Whiskey. It was originally made more than 150 years ago in the Tennessee hills by Nathan "Nearest" Green when he was an enslaved man, and it continued on after he gained his freedom. One of his descendants, Victoria Eady Butler, is Uncle Nearest's master distiller today. This Southern twist on a toddy is a tribute to her and the Green family, who are still making history after all these years. It was inspired by the chocolate we make by the same name that uses these same ingredients. To make this a truly chocolate experience, add a piece of chocolate (or a few cookies) on the side.*

PREP TIME: 5 minutes
COOK TIME: 5 minutes
SERVES: 2

## FOR THE CINNAMON HONEY SIMPLE SYRUP

¼ cup honey

¼ cup water

⅛ teaspoon ground cinnamon

## FOR THE TODDY

4 ounces Uncle Nearest 1856 whiskey

2 ounces unsweet tea

½ ounce cinnamon honey simple syrup

½ ounce lemon juice

2 dehydrated lemon slices, for garnish

Freshly grated nutmeg, for garnish

*Option: Add a lemon twist if you don't have a dehydrated lemon slice.*

## PREPARE THE SIMPLE SYRUP

1. In a small saucepan over medium heat, combine the honey, water, and cinnamon. Cook, stirring frequently, until the honey is completely dissolved.

2. Remove from heat. Let sit for 5 to 10 minutes. Pour through a sieve lined with a cheese cloth into a jar for storage. Let cool before proceeding.

## PREPARE THE TODDY

1. Fill a cocktail mixing glass with ice, then add the whiskey, tea, cinnamon honey simple syrup, and lemon juice. Stir with a cocktail spoon for 15 to 20 seconds.

2. Add one large ice cube or ice sphere to each of two rocks glasses. Pour through a strainer into each glass, and garnish with a dehydrated lemon slice and nutmeg freshly grated using a Microplane.

# Cacao-Infused Old-Fashioned

*We have an old-fashioned truffle in our collection. It combines the classic orange and cherry flavors with rich chocolate. In this cocktail we bring the flavors of that confection into the glass. It's an intriguing way to elevate your whiskey without it being a "dessert" beverage. I selected rye for this as it has a depth and heat that pairs well with the notes of toasted chocolate derived from the cacao nibs.*

## PREPARE THE RYE

1. Start by selecting a high-quality rye that you enjoy. The flavors of the whiskey will be enhanced by the cacao nibs, so choose a whiskey that you like on its own.

2. In a cast-iron skillet over medium heat, toast the cacao nibs for 2 to 3 minutes, until they become fragrant. This will help release the natural oils and intensify the flavor.

3. Add the toasted cacao nibs to a quart glass jar and add the rye. Close the jar tightly. Store the jar in a cool, dark place for at least 48 hours or a few days—depending on the depth of flavor you prefer. Shake the jar gently every so often to agitate the cacao nibs and promote the infusion process.

4. After the desired infusing time, strain the whiskey through a fine-mesh sieve or cheesecloth to remove the cacao nibs. You can transfer the infused rye back into its original bottle or store it in a separate container.

## PREPARE THE OLD-FASHIONED

1. Place 1 orange slice and 1 cherry with 1 teaspoon simple syrup in each of two rocks glasses and muddle to release the flavors.

2. In a mixing glass combine the infused whiskey and bitters.

3. Fill the mixing glass with ice and stir gently with a cocktail spoon for about 30 seconds to chill.

4. Fill the two rocks glasses with ice, then strain the cocktail evenly into them. Garnish with an orange peel and cherry.

*Note: For extra flair, prepare the cocktail, and then smoke it. Make a small cup from aluminum foil and place a teaspoon of dry (not infused) cacao nibs in it. Place the foil next to the prepared cocktail. Carefully light the nibs and cover with a cloche, or place inside a large pot with a lid. The flame will go out and the nibs will smolder. Leave covered for 30 seconds. Voilà! A smoked old-fashioned.*

PREP TIME: 5 minutes, plus at least 2 days of infusing time
SERVES: 2

### FOR THE CACAO-INFUSED RYE

750 milliliters rye whiskey

1 cup cacao nibs

### FOR THE OLD-FASHIONED

2 round slices fresh orange

2 maraschino cherries

2 teaspoons simple syrup

5 ounces cacao-infused rye whiskey

4 dashes Angostura bitters

Skewered orange peel and maraschino cherries, for garnish

*Pro tip: Once you've infused the rye, keep the cacao nibs. You can bake them into cookies or dry them out to grind down and create your own whiskey-infused couverture.*

# White Chocolate Negroni

*Another drink that's been experiencing a renaissance lately, the negroni is a combination of gin, vermouth, and bitter liqueur. Formulating a chocolate version was an especially fun challenge. How do you preserve the cocktail's quintessentially bitter nature while adding a layer of the sweet stuff? It took some experimentation, but the results—which use a white chocolate-washed gin—are undeniably delicious.*

---

**PREP TIME:** 10 minutes, plus 24 to 48 hours of soaking time

**SERVES:** 2

---

### FOR THE WHITE CHOCOLATE-WASHED GIN

1 cup gin

1 cup white chocolate chips, chopped

### FOR THE NEGRONI

2 ounces white chocolate-washed gin

2 ounces sweet vermouth

2 ounces Campari

2 large king ice cubes or ice spheres

Orange twist, for garnish

## PREPARE THE WHITE CHOCOLATE-WASHED GIN

1. Combine the gin and chocolate in a pint mason jar. Screw the lid on tightly and shake vigorously to combine. Store in the refrigerator for 24 to 48 hours, shaking often, to let the flavors meld.

2. Strain the mixture, reserving the gin and discarding the chocolate.

## PREPARE THE COCKTAILS

1. In a shaker filled with ice, combine the gin, vermouth, and Campari. Shake vigorously for 15 to 20 seconds until chilled.

2. Strain into two rocks glasses with large ice cubes. Garnish with orange and serve immediately.

# Smoky Chocolate-Covered Orange Cocktail

*How do you improve on the combination of chocolate and orange? Add a little bit of smoke and a little bit of spice. This spirit-forward mezcal cocktail uses hot honey and chocolate bitters to create a drink that's chocolatey but not overly sweet.*

1. In a small mixing bowl stir the hot honey and hot water together until fully incorporated. If the honey doesn't dissolve, you need hotter water; warm the mixture for 15 seconds in the microwave and stir again. Set aside and let cool slightly.

2. Fill a shaker with ice and add the mezcal, Cointreau, and bitters. Add the hot honey mixture last. Shake well.

3. Add the ice to two rocks glasses and divide the cocktail between the two.

4. Express an orange twist over the top of each cocktail by squeezing the narrow ends together, with the orange side facing the liquor. The essential oils will release over the top. Swipe the orange side around the rim of the glass, and drop the twist into the drink to finish.

PREP TIME: 5 minutes
SERVES: 2

2 teaspoons hot honey

1 teaspoon hot water

3 ounces mezcal

1 ounce orange brandy liqueur (I like Cointreau)

8 dashes chocolate bitters

2 king-sized ice cubes or ice spheres

2 large orange twists

# CHAPTER 8

# Chocolate for Breakfast

**W**here do I think chocolate belongs in breakfast? At the head of the table. Breakfast time was one of the biggest meals of the day in my family because it was before the chaos of the day's duties began, be they school or work. Our morning meal was often biscuits and jam with eggs and some other staple. This was a time when juices were freshly squeezed—although that's a thing again—and bacon still had the rind on it. One of my favorite times growing up, though, was when we were in a hurry and I got to eat Cocoa Pebbles. Gotta love that chocolate milk at the end!

In my book, chocolate isn't just one food; it's a food group. If the whole point of this book is showing the versatility of chocolate and how it's more than just a dessert, this chapter is where the ingredient really shines. If you want to impress your friends, then host a brunch-for-dinner party where you have chocolate in every dish. It will be an evening they'll never forget.

# Cocoa Buttermilk Biscuits

*Biscuits were one of the first things my grandmother Jean taught me to make. This chocolate-infused version can go savory for breakfast or sweet for dessert as a base for strawberry shortcake. (Even better, griddle them.) There's no wrong time to enjoy them.*

1. Preheat the oven to 450 degrees Fahrenheit.

2. In a large mixing bowl sift together the flour, baking powder, and salt.

3. Add the butter to the dry ingredients. Use a pastry cutter, fork, or your fingers to cut the butter into the dry mixture until it resembles coarse crumbs.

4. Melt the chocolate in a small saucepan over medium heat, or in 30-second bursts in the microwave. Allow to cool until cool to the touch but still melted. Whisk in the buttermilk.

5. Make a well in the center of the dry ingredients and pour in the buttermilk mixture. Gently stir until just combined. Do not overmix; the dough should be slightly sticky.

6. Turn the dough out onto a floured surface and knead it gently a few times until it comes together.

7. Roll or pat the dough to ½- to ¾-inch thick.

8. Use a biscuit cutter to cut out biscuits. If you don't have a biscuit cutter, you can use a round glass.

9. Place the biscuits on a baking sheet lined with parchment paper, making sure they're touching slightly for soft sides, or spaced apart for crisper sides. I prefer to cook mine in a cast-iron skillet.

10. Bake in the preheated oven until the biscuits have risen and are lightly browned on top, about 12 to 15 minutes. Allow the biscuits to cool on a wire rack for a few minutes before serving.

11. Serve with butter and jam, or get creative with toppings like whipped cream and chocolate chips.

PREP TIME: 20 minutes
COOK TIME: 15 minutes
YIELDS: 8 to 10

2 cups all-purpose flour

1 tablespoon baking powder

1 teaspoon salt

¼ cup (1 stick) cold unsalted butter, cubed

¾ cup dark chocolate chips

¾ cup buttermilk

# Chocolate Cinnamon Rolls with Cream Cheese Frosting

*Simply put, I am crazy about cinnamon rolls. In my chocolate shop, we make a turtle variation with smoked sea-salted caramel and pecans that is a huge hit with our customers. This cinnamon roll incorporates chocolate in both the dough and the filling, making it the most chocolate cinnamon roll that ever "chocolated."*

## PREPARE THE DOUGH

1. In a large bowl mix together the flour, sugar, cocoa powder, yeast, and salt.

2. In a saucepan heat the milk, butter, and water over medium heat until the butter is melted.

3. Add the milk mixture, eggs, and vanilla to the dry ingredients. Mix until a dough forms.

4. Knead the dough on a floured surface for 5 to 7 minutes, or until smooth and elastic.

5. Place the dough in a lightly oiled bowl, cover with plastic wrap or a towel, and let it rise in a warm place until it doubles in size for about 1 hour.

6. In a small bowl mix together the chocolate, sugar, remaining teaspoon of cocoa, and cinnamon.

7. Roll out the dough into a rectangle. Spread softened butter over the surface of the dough. Sprinkle the chocolate cinnamon sugar mixture evenly over the butter.

8. Starting from the long edge, roll the dough tightly into a log. Cut the log into 12 even pieces.

9. Place the rolls in a greased 9 x 13-inch baking dish. Cover with plastic wrap or a towel and let them rise for another 30 minutes.

10. Preheat the oven to 350 degrees Fahrenheit. Bake the rolls until golden brown, about 20 to 25 minutes. Remove from the oven and allow to cool slightly.

---

PREP TIME: 20 minutes, plus at least 90 minutes rising time
COOK TIME: 25 minutes
YIELDS: 12 rolls

---

## FOR THE CINNAMON ROLLS

3 cups all-purpose flour

1/4 cup granulated sugar

1/2 cup plus 1 teaspoon unsweetened cocoa powder, divided

2 1/4 teaspoons instant active dry yeast (1 package)

1/2 teaspoon salt

1/2 cup whole milk

1/4 cup unsalted butter

1/4 cup water

2 large eggs

1 teaspoon vanilla extract

1/2 cup semisweet chocolate, chopped fine

1/3 cup granulated sugar

1 tablespoon ground cinnamon

1/4 cup (1/2 stick) unsalted butter, softened

## FOR THE CREAM CHEESE FROSTING

¼ cup milk chocolate chips

8 ounces (1 brick) cream cheese, softened

½ cup (1 stick) unsalted butter, softened

1 cup confectioners' sugar

½ teaspoon vanilla extract

2 to 3 tablespoons milk

## PREPARE THE FROSTING

1. Melt the chocolate chips in a small saucepan over medium heat or in 30-second bursts in the microwave. Allow to cool until the chocolate is cooled but still melted.

2. In a small bowl or a stand mixer fitted with a paddle attachment, beat the cream cheese and butter until smooth. Add the chocolate and mix until incorporated. Add the confectioners' sugar and vanilla, mixing until fully combined. Stream in milk to reach desired consistency, taking care not to make it too thin.

3. Once the rolls have cooled, generously spread the frosting over each and enjoy!

# Turtle Cheesecake Baked French Toast

*If a recipe title has "turtle" in it, sign me up. Add turtle to French toast and I'm lost. I love using brioche and challah breads for my French toast as they create such a decadent, pleasing dish. The cream cheese filling adds another dimension of flavor that won't soon be forgotten. Serve this indulgent, sweet breakfast with savory meats on the side. Even better, add a mimosa or two.*

## PREPARE THE FRENCH TOAST

1. Grease a 9 x 13-inch baking dish with butter or cooking spray. Cube the bread and spread half evenly in the dish.

2. In a medium bowl beat the cream cheese and ½ cup of the granulated sugar until smooth and creamy.

3. In a large mixing bowl whisk together the eggs, remaining ½ cup of the granulated sugar, milk, heavy cream, vanilla, ground cinnamon, and salt until well combined.

4. Pour half of the custard mixture over half of the cubed bread, ensuring all pieces are soaked. Dollop the cream cheese mixture over the soaked bread and use a spatula to spread it out as evenly as possible. Sprinkle the mini chocolate chips and pecans over the top.

5. Place the remaining cubed bread over the first layer and pour the remaining custard mixture over the top, ensuring all bread pieces are soaked. Press down lightly with a spatula to help the bread absorb the custard.

6. Cover the baking dish with plastic wrap or aluminum foil and refrigerate for at least 2 hours, or overnight for best results.

7. Preheat the oven to 325 degrees Fahrenheit. Remove the French toast from the refrigerator, and let it sit at room temperature while the oven preheats.

8. Bake, uncovered, for 55 to 60 minutes, or until the top is golden brown and the custard is set.

**PREP TIME:** 15 minutes, plus at least 2 hours chilling time
**COOK TIME:** 60 minutes
**SERVES:** 8 to10

## FOR THE FRENCH TOAST

1 loaf (about 1½ pounds) brioche or challah

8 ounces (1 brick) cream cheese, softened

1 cup granulated sugar, divided

4 large eggs

1½ cups whole milk

½ cup heavy cream

2 teaspoons vanilla extract

1 teaspoon ground cinnamon

¼ teaspoon salt

¾ cup mini chocolate chips

1 cup chopped pecans

## PREPARE THE TOPPING

1. While the French toast is baking, prepare the topping. Place the sugar in a heavy-bottomed pot over medium-high heat.

2. In a separate saucepan mix the heavy cream, vanilla, and sea salt over medium heat and warm to just before boiling, about 3 minutes. Remove from heat.

3. Once the sugar has melted and turned amber in color, after about 5 minutes, remove from the heat and pour in the cream mixture. Allow to bubble, then stir well to combine.

4. Pour caramel into a jar through a sieve to remove any small clumps of sugar.

## ASSEMBLE FRENCH TOAST

1. Once baked, remove the French toast from the oven and let it cool slightly.

2. Drizzle the caramel sauce over the top. Dust with confectioners' sugar, or top with a dollop of whipped cream for an extra touch.

### FOR THE TOPPING

1 cup granulated sugar

1 cup heavy cream

1 teaspoon vanilla extract

1/4 teaspoon sea salt

Confectioners' sugar for dusting or whipped cream for garnish

_____

*Option: Instead of cubing the bread in the first step, layer slices like fallen dominoes and layer the stuffing in between the slices, then proceed with the regular assembling.*

# Triple Chocolate Bread Pudding

*What started as a poor man's dessert is now one of the most deliciously comforting treats around. This luxe version of bread pudding could easily work after dinner, especially topped with ice cream, but it works equally well as a breakfast dish. Pro tip: The leftovers make the best French toast you've ever had.*

1. Using a serrated bread knife, cut loaf of bread into medium to large cubes. Place in a large bowl and let sit uncovered while preparing the other ingredients. (The recipe works best when the bread is stale, so do this the day before if possible.)

2. In the bowl of a stand mixer fitted with a paddle attachment, combine the egg yolks, sugar, vanilla, and salt. Beat on medium speed until fully combined, about 1 minute.

3. Add the cocoa powder and mix briefly. While the mixer is going, stream in the cream and milk.

4. Pour the cocoa mixture over the cubed bread, then fold until the bread is evenly coated. Cover with plastic wrap and refrigerate for at least 1 hour or overnight to allow the bread to fully soak up all the liquid.

5. Preheat the oven to 400 degrees Fahrenheit.

6. Grease a 9 x 13-inch baking dish with the softened butter. Remove the fully soaked bread from the refrigerator. Fold in both kinds of chocolate chips and transfer all contents into the prepared dish. Bake for 45 to 60 minutes, until the top looks fully cooked and the center has risen. Remove from the oven and set the pan on a cooling rack. Allow it to cool for 10 to 15 minutes.

7. Spoon into bowls and serve hot with Rum Butter Caramel Sauce.

---

**PREP TIME:** 15 minutes, plus soaking time
**COOK TIME:** 60 minutes
**SERVES:** 12

---

1 loaf (about 1½ pounds) brioche or challah

8 large egg yolks

1 cup granulated sugar

1 teaspoon vanilla extract

¼ teaspoon salt

1½ cups unsweetened cocoa powder

4 cups heavy cream

2 cups whole milk

1 tablespoon unsalted butter, softened

1 cup semisweet chocolate chips

1 cup milk chocolate chips

Rum Butter Caramel Sauce (see page 227) for serving

# Chocolate Strawberry Dutch Baby

*This recipe is a sweet breakfast or brunch dish that combines the classic Dutch baby pancake with fresh strawberries and chocolate. The Dutch baby is a large, puffy pancake that is cooked in a cast-iron skillet in the oven and is often served with powdered sugar, lemon juice, and fresh fruit. I have my great-grandmother's cast-iron skillet that was passed down from my grandmother to my mother and then me, so I am always creating recipes for it. You are going to love this chocolatey, custardy version of a brunch classic.*

**PREP TIME:** 10 minutes
**COOK TIME:** 25 minutes
**SERVES:** 4

3 large eggs

½ cup all-purpose flour

¼ cup unsweetened cocoa powder

½ cup whole milk

½ teaspoon vanilla extract

¼ teaspoon salt

1¼ cups sliced fresh strawberries, divided

2 tablespoons unsalted butter

¼ cup chopped dark chocolate

Confectioners' sugar, for serving

1. Preheat the oven to 425 degrees Fahrenheit.

2. In a large bowl whisk together the eggs, flour, cocoa powder, milk, vanilla, and salt until smooth.

3. Gently fold 1 cup of the fresh strawberries into the pancake batter.

4. Over medium heat melt the butter in a cast-iron skillet. Swirl the butter around to coat the bottom and sides of the skillet.

5. Pour the pancake batter into the skillet and sprinkle the chopped chocolate on top.

6. Place the skillet in the preheated oven and bake until the pancake is puffed and golden brown, about 20 to 25 minutes.

7. Remove the skillet from the oven and sprinkle the remaining sliced strawberries on top of the pancake.

8. Dust the top of the pancake with confectioners' sugar.

9. Slice it into wedges like a pie and serve hot.

# Chocolate Liege Waffles

*Waffles are one of my favorite breakfast foods. I started making them in college because they were quick but something I could still make from scratch. To this day, I keep a waffle iron in the house. I love them so much, I made a version of this recipe, dipped each waffle in dark chocolate, and sold them in my chocolate shop. They were a hot item. This recipe works for brunch or dessert and could become a regular in your kitchen.*

1. To activate the yeast, in a small bowl, combine the warm milk, active dry yeast, and 1 tablespoon of the granulated sugar. Let it sit for about 5 to 10 minutes, until it becomes frothy.

2. In the bowl of a stand mixer fitted with the paddle attachment, beat the eggs. Add the butter, vanilla, remaining granulated sugar, and salt. Mix until combined. Gradually add the flour and the yeast mixture to the bowl, mixing on low speed until a dough forms.

3. Switch to the dough hook attachment and knead the dough on medium speed until it is smooth and elastic, about 5 minutes.

4. Cover the bowl with plastic wrap or a clean kitchen towel, and let the dough rise in a warm place until it has doubled in size, about 1½ to 2 hours.

5. Once the dough has risen, gently fold in the pearl sugar and chopped chocolate until evenly distributed.

6. Divide the dough into 10 to 12 equal portions and shape each portion into a ball. Place the balls on a baking sheet lined with parchment paper.

7. Cover the dough balls with a clean kitchen towel and let them rise for another 30 to 45 minutes.

8. Preheat the waffle iron.

9. Place a dough ball in the center of the waffle iron, and cook until the waffle is golden brown and caramelized, about 3 to 5 minutes. The exact cooking time may vary depending on your waffle iron.

10. Serve the waffles plain or topped with whipped cream, fresh berries, or a drizzle of Chocolate Caramel Sauce (see page 224).

**PREP TIME**: 20 minutes, plus at least 2 hours rising time
**COOK TIME**: 5 minutes
**YIELDS**: 10 to 12 waffles

½ cup whole milk, warmed to about 110 degrees Fahrenheit

2¼ teaspoons (1 packet) active dry yeast

3 tablespoons granulated sugar, divided

2 large eggs

1 cup (2 sticks) unsalted butter, softened

2 teaspoons vanilla extract

½ teaspoon salt

3⅔ cups all-purpose flour

1 cup pearl sugar

1 cup chopped dark chocolate

Berries, whipped cream, or caramel sauce, optional, for garnish

213

# Candied Bacon Figs

*In Memphis, backyards are full of fig trees, but in my view, you don't see the fruit used often enough on menus. These delicious bites are the ideal balance of sweet and savory, with a big punch of flavor from the bacon, perfectly lightened by the sweetness of figs and chocolate. Pro tip: Make a double batch. They're going to disappear quickly.*

**PREP TIME:** 15 minutes, plus setting time
**COOK TIME:** 25 minutes
**YIELDS:** 24 pieces

½ cup firmly packed light brown sugar

¼ teaspoon paprika

Pinch of chili powder

¼ teaspoon garlic powder

¼ teaspoon onion powder

Pinch of salt

Pinch of dry mustard

Pinch of cayenne pepper

12 slices bacon, sliced in half into shorter strips

12 fresh figs, halved

½ cup tempered dark chocolate

*Option: Stuff with either goat cheese or blue cheese for a variation.*

1. Preheat the oven to 375 degrees Fahrenheit. Line a baking sheet with parchment paper and fit with a baking rack.

2. In a small bowl mix together the brown sugar, paprika, chili powder, garlic powder, onion powder, salt, dry mustard, and cayenne pepper.

3. Working in batches, spread the bacon strips on a paper towel–lined, microwave-safe plate, and microwave the bacon for 1 to 2 minutes to partially cook it.

4. Wrap each fig half with a piece of bacon, securing with a toothpick.

5. Roll the bacon-wrapped figs in the brown sugar mixture, making sure to coat them evenly.

6. Place the coated figs on the prepared baking sheet, spacing them apart so they don't touch.

7. Bake for 20 to 25 minutes, or until the bacon is crispy and the figs are tender.

8. Melt the chocolate in a small saucepan over medium heat, or in the microwave in 30-second bursts.

9. Remove the figs from the oven and let them cool slightly. Drizzle with the melted chocolate and serve warm.

# Hot Honey Jalapeño Chocolate Cornbread with Cinnamon Butter

*I'm a firm believer that anything can be breakfast if you believe it can—and adding chocolate helps. This savory-sweet skillet cornbread is just as delicious on the dinner table as it is with morning coffee, especially when topped with this freshly made cinnamon butter. Homemade butter is shockingly easy to make, but if you're looking for an even easier option, you can just melt a stick of butter, mix in the cinnamon and sugar, and cool it down to a solid state again.*

## PREPARE THE CORNBREAD

1. Preheat the oven to 400 degrees Fahrenheit. Grease a 10-inch cast-iron skillet. Line the bottom of the skillet with the jalapeño slices and pour the honey over them.

2. In a large mixing bowl combine the flour, cornmeal, cocoa powder, sugar, and baking powder.

3. Melt the butter in the microwave or on the stovetop.

4. In a medium mixing bowl whisk together the melted butter, buttermilk, and eggs. Stir the liquids into the dry ingredients until just moistened, then add chocolate chips.

5. Pour the batter into the skillet. Bake for 20 minutes, or until a knife inserted into the center of the cornbread comes out clean. Remove from the oven.

## PREPARE THE CINNAMON BUTTER

1. Place the cream in a 4-cup measuring cup or other sturdy container with tall sides and mix with an immersion blender until the butter fat starts to solidify and separate from the liquids, about 4 minutes.

2. Remove the immersion blender, then, using a rubber spatula or wooden spoon, press the solid butter against the sides of the cup and drain the excess liquid. Continue the process until the butter has stopped producing liquid.

3. Place the butter in a bowl with a lid. Stir in the cinnamon, sugar, and salt, cover, and refrigerate until ready to use.

4. Serve the cornbread warm with the butter, or griddle slices of the cornbread in melted butter and add a sprinkle of brown sugar.

PREP TIME: 15 minutes
COOK TIME: 20 minutes
SERVES: 8 to 10

## FOR THE CORNBREAD

1 jalapeño, seeded and sliced into rings

1/4 cup hot honey

1 cup all-purpose flour

1 1/2 cups cornmeal

1/4 cup unsweetened cocoa powder

1/4 cup granulated sugar

2 teaspoons baking powder

8 tablespoons unsalted butter, plus more for greasing

1 cup buttermilk

2 large eggs

3/4 cup semisweet chocolate chips

## FOR THE CINNAMON BUTTER

2 cups heavy cream, room temperature

1/2 teaspoon cinnamon

1 teaspoon granulated sugar

Pinch of salt

# Chocolate Soufflé Pancakes with Matcha Glaze and Pear Sake–Infused Whipped Cream

*Soufflé pancakes are just pure fun. Not only do they make a dramatic presentation with their exaggerated stature, they elicit over-the-top reactions with their decadent texture. This is my tribute to the Japanese soufflé pancake, using earthy green tea matcha and sweet pear sake. If you'd rather skip the sake, just add a ½ teaspoon vanilla extract instead.*

## PREPARE THE PANCAKES

1. In a mixing bowl whisk together the egg yolks, milk, and vanilla extract until well combined.

2. Sift in the flour, baking soda, and cocoa powder, then whisk until smooth.

3. In a separate bowl use an electric mixer to beat the egg whites and cream of tartar until foamy.

4. Gradually add the granulated sugar while continuing to beat until stiff peaks form.

5. Gently fold the egg whites into the chocolate mixture in thirds, being careful not to deflate the batter.

6. Heat a nonstick skillet over low heat and add a small amount of butter.

7. Spoon the batter into the skillet, using about ¼ cup per pancake. Cook covered for 3 to 4 minutes on each side, or until the pancakes are set and lightly browned.

8. Transfer the cooked pancakes to a plate and keep warm in a low oven while you prepare the glaze.

## PREPARE THE GLAZE

1. In a bowl whisk together the confectioners' sugar and matcha powder.

2. Gradually add the milk, whisking until you achieve a smooth, pourable consistency.

---

**PREP TIME:** 20 minutes
**COOK TIME:** 20 minutes
**YIELDS:** 12 pancakes

---

### FOR THE SOUFFLÉ PANCAKES

3 large egg yolks

¼ cup milk

1 teaspoon vanilla extract

½ cup all-purpose flour

1 teaspoon baking soda

2 tablespoons unsweetened cocoa powder

4 large egg whites

¼ teaspoon cream of tartar

¼ cup granulated sugar

2 tablespoons unsalted butter (for cooking)

### FOR THE MATCHA GLAZE

1 cup confectioners' sugar

2 teaspoons matcha powder

2 to 3 tablespoons milk

## FOR THE PEAR SAKE–INFUSED WHIPPED CREAM

1 cup heavy whipping cream

2 tablespoons pear sake

2 tablespoons confectioners' sugar

1 teaspoon vanilla extract

## PREPARE THE WHIPPED CREAM

1. In the chilled bowl of a stand mixer fitted with a whip, combine the heavy cream, pear sake, confectioners' sugar, and vanilla.

2. Beat until soft peaks form.

## ASSEMBLE THE PANCAKES

1. Stack the chocolate soufflé pancakes on serving plates.

2. Generously drizzle the matcha glaze over the pancakes. Add a dollop of pear sake–infused whipped cream on top of the pancakes.

# CHAPTER 9

# Frostings, Glazes, Sauces, and Garnishes

The magic of a dish lies in the details—the final flourish that turns a meal into an experience, a treat into a memory. We eat with our eyes first, and those finishing touches are what captivate us, drawing us into a moment that feels as special as it looks. Think of a swirl of whipped cream that brings lightness to a dessert or a sprinkle of sea salt that makes each bite sing. Picture that swipe of fresh butter melting into warm, crusty bread, leaving a taste that lingers long after the meal.

True artisanship in the kitchen is about honoring every flavor, texture, and sensation, transforming ingredients into art. Each element—whether a drizzle of caramel over cake or a touch of zest on a delicate pastry—adds dimension and depth. A dish might be good without them, but these finishing touches elevate it, bringing perfection within reach. It's here, in the final details, where mastery and passion converge, turning the ordinary into the unforgettable.

# Perfect Caramel (or Chocolate Caramel) Sauce

*There are competing schools of thought about the best way to make caramel, but I prefer the dry method. It takes a little bit of practice, so make sure you have enough ingredients on hand to make a second batch when you're first learning. It's easier than you might think to burn the caramel—and you'll need to start over—but once you've got the technique down, you'll be whipping up fresh caramel all the time.*

PREP TIME: 5 minutes
COOK TIME: 10 minutes
YIELDS: 2½ cups

2 cups granulated sugar

1 cup heavy cream

1 tablespoon vanilla bean paste

½ teaspoon kosher salt

½ cup light corn syrup

4 ounces dark chocolate chunks, optional

1. In a heavy-bottomed pot heat the sugar over high heat. Once it has begun melting, gently move the sugar around to prevent scorching. Do this as little as possible; don't fully stir it.

2. When the sugar has the consistency of wet sand, after about 2 minutes, reduce heat to medium. Continue to move sugar around a bit, breaking up any clumps. After another 2 minutes, once the sugar is about 90 percent melted, turn off the heat and allow the residual heat to finish melting it, about 2 to 3 minutes.

3. While the sugar is cooking, combine the cream, vanilla, salt, and corn syrup in a small saucepan over medium heat. Warm the mixture until just before boiling and stir well.

4. Slowly pour the cream mixture into the hot caramel. Give the sugar only about 2 to 3 minutes off the heat before doing this, or it will burn. Let bubbles settle, then stir with a whisk until well combined. Pour through a sieve or strainer to remove any remaining sugar clumps.

5. If you're making chocolate caramel sauce, when the caramel is warm but not hot, stir in the chocolate chunks until melted. Blend with an immersion blender to smooth out the texture.

6. Serve warm or store in a container with a lid in the refrigerator for up to 2 weeks.

# Rum Butter Caramel Sauce

*This sauce takes classic caramel and elevates it to another stratosphere. If you want to add a touch of vanilla bean paste as I do when making basic caramel, I wouldn't be mad at you, but I really want the rum to take the lead here. You should end up with a silky, thick, rich, and slightly boozy caramel that will elevate almost any dessert.*

1. Set a heavy-bottomed pot on high heat for 2 or 3 minutes, until very hot. Place the sugar in the pot. There may be some smoking as the dry substance hits the hot pot, but no need to panic. Just turn your vent on, and you'll be fine.

2. As the sugar begins to melt, move it around very slowly and gently with a wooden spoon—avoid rigorous stirring—so that it cooks evenly without burning in spots and there are no chunks of sugar remaining.

3. About midway through, turn the heat down to medium low. Once the sugar has begun to melt, the residual heat will do much of the work for you. Keep your eye on the caramel so it doesn't darken too quickly, and adjust the heat as needed.

4. Meanwhile, in a small pot, heat the cream, salt, and rum on medium heat just until hot, about 3 minutes, stirring to combine.

5. Once the caramel is a deep amber color, pour the rum-cream mixture into the caramel and stir until fully combined. Turn the heat off, add the butter, and stir once more. Serve warm, or store in the refrigerator in a covered container for up to 2 weeks.

PREP TIME: 5 minutes
COOK TIME: 15 minutes
YIELDS: 2½ cups

2¼ cups granulated sugar

¾ cup heavy cream

½ teaspoon kosher salt

¼ cup dark rum

1 tablespoon unsalted butter, chilled

# Praline Nuts

*These sweet (and if you want, spiced) nuts are a delicious snack on their own, and the perfect happy hour snack or a much-welcomed addition to a charcuterie board. Better yet, use them to add another dimension to pancakes, cookies, brownies . . . anything that would benefit from a touch of rich, nutty depth. You could even whip up a batch and then blend it in the food processor to make a paste to use in fillings (or the best PB&J you've ever had).*

**PREP TIME:** 10 minutes
**COOK TIME:** 20 minutes
**YIELDS:** 2 cups

¾ cup granulated sugar

¼ cup water

¼ teaspoon salt

2 cups nuts (pecans, walnuts, almonds, cashews, or a combination)

½ teaspoon vanilla extract

¼ teaspoon ground cinnamon or cardamom, optional

1. Preheat the oven to 350 degrees Fahrenheit. Line a baking sheet with parchment paper or a silicone mat.

2. In a medium-sized saucepan combine the sugar, water, and salt. Cook over medium heat, stirring occasionally, until the sugar has dissolved and the mixture comes to a boil.

3. Add the nuts to the saucepan and stir to coat them evenly with the sugar syrup. Continue to cook for 3 to 4 minutes, stirring constantly, until the syrup thickens slightly.

4. Remove the saucepan from heat and stir in the vanilla and any optional spices you'd like to add.

5. Using a slotted spoon or tongs, transfer the coated nuts to the prepared baking sheet, spreading them out in a single layer.

6. Bake in the preheated oven until the nuts are golden brown and fragrant, about 10 to 15 minutes. Keep an eye on them to prevent burning.

7. Remove the baking sheet from the oven and let the candied praline nuts cool completely. As they cool, they will harden and become crunchy.

8. Once cooled, store the candied praline nuts in an airtight container at room temperature for up to 2 weeks.

# Tanghulu "Glass" Strawberries

*This trendy snack—fresh fruit made even more vibrant by dipping it in crystal-clear candy syrup—originated in China. It works with many kinds of fruit, makes a beautiful dessert on its own, and elevates other desserts to a whole new level. Use this as a topping on the Black Velvet Cake (see page 147) or Blackout Chocolate Cake (see page 137), or even on the Triple Chocolate Bread Pudding (see page 209) or Turtle Cheesecake Baked French Toast (see page 205).*

1. Prepare your strawberries by washing and drying them thoroughly. Remove leaves and cut stems down to the base. Depending on how you plan on using them, either put one strawberry on the end of a skewer or stack 2 or 3 berries on one stick.

2. Prepare a place to dry your dipped tanghulu. A brick of Styrofoam works well, or poke small holes in an empty box in which to place the skewers so they can stand up to dry and preserve their shape.

3. In a small saucepan combine the sugar and water. Heat over medium heat until the sugar has completely dissolved, come to a boil, and reached a light amber color (300 degrees Fahrenheit on a candy thermometer). Remove from heat and let the syrup cool for a few minutes.

4. With one hand tilting the pot to create a deeper pool of syrup, use your other hand to dip each strawberry into the syrup, making sure to coat it fully. Allow any excess syrup to drip off, then insert the other end of the skewer into your prepared brick or box. This allows the syrup to set without any indentations or flat sides.

5. Repeat the dipping process with all the strawberries as quickly as possible so the syrup doesn't become too thick. Let them sit at room temperature for 20 to 30 minutes to allow the syrup to harden.

6. Once the syrup has hardened, you can serve the tanghulu immediately or refrigerate it for up to 2 days.

**PREP TIME:** 15 minutes, plus 30 minutes setting time
**COOK TIME:** 5 minutes
**YIELDS:** 12 berries

12 strawberries
Skewers
1½ cups granulated sugar
¾ cup water

# Chocolate Bowls

*I learned this neat trick years ago, and it always makes a big impression. You can really get fancy and lace your chocolate with an alternate couverture to create a marbled effect.*

PREP TIME: 10 minutes

YIELDS: 4 bowls

Balloons

1 cup Couverture chocolate
(dark, milk, white, or a combo)

1. Inflate the balloons to your desired cup size, ensuring they are clean and dry. Tie them off.

2. Temper the chocolate using the seeding method (see page 39).

3. Line a baking sheet or tray with parchment paper.

4. Dip the bottom half of each inflated balloon into the melted chocolate, ensuring that it is evenly coated. Dip twice to ensure chocolate is thick enough. You can also dip at an angle on all sides, creating a tulip effect.

5. Place the chocolate-coated balloons onto the paper-lined tray and let them set in the refrigerator for 15 to 20 minutes, or until the chocolate hardens.

6. Once the chocolate has hardened, gently deflate the balloons by releasing the air slowly. The chocolate cups should easily separate from the balloons.

7. Carefully remove the deflated balloons from the chocolate cups, making sure not to break the chocolate shell.

8. Your chocolate cups are now ready to be filled with dessert or treats.

# Golden Syrup

*Golden syrup is more common in Europe than it is in the US, and it's a great alternative to corn syrup. It stabilizes texture in a similar way but doesn't have the same high-fructose composition. You can order golden syrup online or find it in some specialty stores, but it's just as easy to make it yourself and store at room temperature until you need it.*

1. In a heavy-bottomed saucepan add 1 cup of the granulated sugar and ¼ cup of the water. Stir to combine.

2. Heat the mixture over medium heat, stirring constantly until the sugar dissolves and turns a deep amber color. This process will take 5 to 10 minutes. Be careful not to let it burn.

3. Once the sugar has caramelized, briefly remove from heat. Carefully add the remaining water to the saucepan. The mixture will bubble up vigorously, so pour slowly and stand back to avoid splattering. Note: Removing from the heat and adding warm water helps to reduce the bubbling.

4. Add the remaining granulated sugar and the lemon juice to the pot. Stir until the sugar is completely dissolved.

5. Reduce the heat to low and let the mixture simmer gently for about 45 minutes to 1 hour, stirring occasionally until a candy thermometer measures 230 degrees Fahrenheit. The syrup will thicken as it cooks. You want to achieve a consistency similar to maple syrup.

6. To check the consistency, dip a spoon into the syrup and let it cool slightly. The syrup should coat the spoon and have a slow, steady drip.

7. Once the syrup has reached the desired consistency, let it cool slightly in the pan. Pour the syrup into clean, sterilized jars or bottles, and let it cool completely before sealing. The syrup will thicken further as it cools to a consistency similar to honey. Store the golden syrup in a cool, dark place. It can be kept for several months.

**PREP TIME:** 5 minutes
**COOK TIME:** 70 minutes
**YIELDS:** 6 cups

4 cups granulated sugar, divided

1½ cups water, divided

2 teaspoons lemon juice

# Homemade Pie Crust

*I will never judge anyone for using a premade pie crust, or any shortcut that saves you some time in the kitchen. But if you're a "homemade or it never happened" person, here's an easy recipe. If you're making a pie that calls for only one crust, split the dough equally, then wrap half in plastic wrap and freeze it for next time. If you want to make this a chocolate crust, add 2 tablespoons of cocoa powder to the dry ingredients.*

---

**PREP TIME:** 10 minutes, plus at least 30 minutes chilling time

**YIELDS:** 2 crusts

---

2½ cups all-purpose flour

1 teaspoon sugar

1 teaspoon salt

1¼ cups (2½ sticks) unsalted butter, chilled and cubed

¼ cup to ½ cup ice water

1. In the bowl of a food processor fitted with a blade, combine the flour, sugar, and salt. Pulse to combine.

2. Add the butter and mix in the food processor until the mixture is in lumps the size of peas. Continue to mix while adding ice water 1 tablespoon at a time until the dough has combined but isn't too wet. You likely won't need all the water.

3. Remove from the food processor, divide into two, wrap each half in plastic wrap, and refrigerate the dough for at least 30 minutes. When you're ready, roll one half on a floured surface and follow the directions of your recipe.

# Bourbon-Washed Butter

*Using a fat-like butter to "wash" a spirit like bourbon creates a savory richness in cocktails and has become increasingly popular with mixologists of late. This method has two benefits: You have enhanced bourbon for sipping, and you have spirit-infused butter to use in frostings or anywhere else you think a dessert would be elevated by having a tinge of whiskey flavor.*

1. Grate the butter and place in a 16-ounce mason jar.

2. Pour the bourbon over the butter. Seal the jar and place it in the refrigerator for 24 to 48 hours. Gently shake periodically.

3. Using a cheesecloth and a sieve, separate the butter and bourbon into separate jars. Seal each jar and keep both in the refrigerator until ready to use.

**PREP TIME:** 10 minutes, plus at least 24 hours chilling time

**YIELDS:** 1 cup butter and 7 ounces bourbon

1 cup (2 sticks) unsalted butter, chilled or frozen

8 ounces bourbon

# CHAPTER 10

# For the Love of Eating (and Drinking) Chocolate

**A**s I mentioned before, I think of chocolate as a food group, one that can work in every meal and belongs at every table. Hopefully by this point in the book, you've embraced the full possibilities of chocolate as well. But when you're putting together a menu that's heavy on chocolate—or just dreaming up new recipes to try out—it's important to remember what flavor profiles work best with which chocolates so you know how to integrate them into your menus. That's how you create depth and nuance: by layering contrasting yet complementary flavors. Experimenting with flavors and textures, just like the character did in *Charlie and the Chocolate Factory*, is what really makes me feel like the real-life Willy Wonka. I hope you'll take some risks and try out some unexpected combinations too.

Here's a brief rundown of pairing notes for when you're ready to experiment. I've not only arranged pairings of foods, wines, and spirits, but I've also followed those with menu pairings from recipes in the book to make your guests want to come back for more!

# The Art of Pairings

Pairing chocolate is both an art and a science. Much of my approach to it is derived from experiences over time. It's really all about storytelling—creating a narrative with chocolate and food, and having a love for the people with whom I get to share.

## White Chocolate

**TASTING NOTES:** butter, cream, vanilla

**COMPLEMENTARY FLAVORS:** berries (raspberry, cranberry), citrus (lemon, orange, yuzu), herbs (rosemary, thyme), white balsamic vinegar, almond, tea (jasmine, green)

**WINE PAIRINGS:** sparkling rosé, Gewürztraminer, dry Riesling, Picpoul de Pinet, Beaujolais

**SPIRITS PAIRINGS:** white distilled spirits (vodka, gin, white rum, tequila blanco)

## Blonde Chocolate

**TASTING NOTES:** toast, caramel

**COMPLEMENTARY FLAVORS:** cookie butter, hazelnut, vanilla, honey, brown sugar, seeded fruit (apple, pear)

**WINE PAIRINGS:** Cava, Chablis, sherry

**SPIRITS PAIRINGS:** brandy, cognac, cask-distilled spirits

## Ruby Chocolate

**TASTING NOTES:** berry, mild tartness

**COMPLEMENTARY FLAVORS:** berries (blueberry, strawberry), citrus (blood orange, mandarin), papaya, persimmon, wildflower honey, tea (chamomile, rosehip)

**WINE PAIRINGS:** rosé, port, Lambrusco, Bordeaux, grenache

**SPIRITS PAIRINGS:** spirits distilled from fruit (grappa, moonshine)

## Milk Chocolate

**TASTING NOTES:** vanilla, caramel, cocoa, milk

**COMPLEMENTARY FLAVORS:** smoke (bacon, hickory), herbs (basil, mint), stone fruit (peach, apricot), warm spices (nutmeg, cinnamon, star anise, cayenne), orange blossom honey, pineapple, tea (Earl Grey, Irish breakfast)

**WINE PAIRINGS:** champagne, pinot noir, merlot, Syrah

**SPIRITS PAIRINGS:** cask-distilled spirits (bourbon, whiskey, spiced or aged rum, tequila añejo)

## Dark Chocolate

**TASTING NOTES:** floral, earthy

**COMPLEMENTARY FLAVORS:** espresso, sea salt, root vegetables (sweet potato, parsnip, beet), earthy spices (cumin, clove, peppercorn), dark fruits (date, raisin, prune, fig)

**WINE PAIRINGS:** Chianti, zinfandel, Malbec, cabernet sauvignon

**SPIRITS PAIRINGS:** smoky spirits (scotch, mezcal), bourbon and rye, tequila reposado, aged rum

# Build Your Own Chocuterie Spread

I've said it before and I'll say it again: I believe chocolate belongs at the head of the table, no matter what kind of meal you're serving. Here are some suggested menus for chocolate-filled meals.

## Chocolate for Breakfast

Chocolate Pineapple Upside-Down Cake with Grand Marnier-Brown Butter
    Caramel
Chocolate Strawberry Dutch Baby
Chocolate Soufflé Pancakes with Matcha Glaze and Pear Sake–Infused
    Whipped Cream
Candied Bacon Figs
Turtle Cheesecake Baked French Toast

## A Chocuterie Feast

Campfire S'mores Fudge
"Billionaire" Chocolate Praline Shortbread
Chocolate Butter Pecan Toffee
Fried Chocolate Hand Pies
Chocolate Barbecue Popcorn
Mississippi Mud Hot Chocolate

## Springtime Soiree

Key Lime White Chocolate Pudding in Chocolate Bowls
White Chocolate Hummingbird Cake Pops with Candied Ginger
Chocolate Banana Pudding Torte
Vegan Avocado Chocolate Pudding
Smoky Chocolate-Covered Orange Cocktail

## A Summertime Spread

Strawberries and Champagne White Chocolate Fudge

Blue Cheese Shortbread with White Chocolate Drizzle

Big Island Cookies

Black Velvet Cake with Tanghulu "Glass" Strawberries

Uncle Nearest Queen V Toddy

All-Pink-Everything Sparkling Cocktail

## Autumn Harvest Meal

Chocolate Sourdough Brioche

Peanut Butter Caramel Cayenne Brownies

Sweet Potato Sticky Toffee Pudding

Friendsgiving Chocolate Pecan Pie

Chocolate Memphian Cocktail

## Holiday Celebration

Chocolate-Dipped Marshmallow Cookie

Dinner Party Cheesecake-Stuffed Cookies

Chocolate Sweet Potato Pie with Brown Sugar Meringue

Cherry Cordial Gelato

Cacao-Infused Old-Fashioned

# Notes

## Introduction

1. "Juicy," by The Notorious B.I.G., track 10 on *Ready to Die* (Diddy and Poke, 1994).
2. Mel Stuart, dir., *Willy Wonka and the Chocolate Factory* (Warner Bros., 1971).

## Chapter 1: Chocistry 101

1. Elizabeth LaBau, "What Is Dark Chocolate?" The Spruce Eats, updated January 1, 2024, https://www.thespruceeats.com/dark-chocolate-520354.
2. Elizabeth LaBau, "Common Chocolate Types and Varieties," The Spruce Eats, updated April 14, 2023, https://www.thespruceeats.com/a-guide-to-chocolate-varieties-520311.
3. LaBau, "Common Chocolate Types and Varieties."
4. Pamela Vachon, "What Is Ruby Chocolate & What Makes It Pink?" The Chocolate Professor, April 12, 2023, https://www.thechocolateprofessor.com/blog/ruby-chocolate.
5. Sonia Zarrillo et al., "The Use and Domestication of *Theobroma cacao* During the Mid-Holocene in the Upper Amazon," *Nature Ecology & Evolution* 2 (October 29, 2018), https://doi.org/10.1038/s41559–018–0697-x.
6. Amanda Fiegl, "A Brief History of Chocolate," *Smithsonian* magazine, March 1, 2008, https://www.smithsonianmag.com/arts-culture/a-brief-history-of-chocolate-21860917.
7. Fiegl, "A Brief History of Chocolate."
8. Veronika Barišić et al., "The Chemistry Behind Chocolate Production," *Molecules* 24, no. 17 (2019), https://doi.org/10.3390/molecules24173163.
9. Fiegl, "A Brief History of Chocolate."
10. Sophie D. Coe and Michael D. Coe, *The True History of Chocolate*, 3rd ed. (Thames & Hudson, 2013).
11. Fiegl, "A Brief History of Chocolate."
12. "Unwrap the Fascinating Story of Chocolate Through the Ages," American Heritage Chocolate, https://www.americanheritagechocolate.com/history-of-chocolate.
13. Fiegl, "A Brief History of Chocolate."
14. Donatella Lippi, "Chocolate in History: Food, Medicine, Medi-Food," *Nutrients* 5, no. 5 (2013), https://doi.org/10.3390/nu5051573.
15. Fiegl, "A Brief History of Chocolate."
16. Lippi, "Chocolate in History: Food, Medicine, Medi-Food."
17. Teresa L. Dillinger et al., "Food of the Gods: Cure for Humanity? A Cultural History of the Medicinal and Ritual Use of Chocolate," *The Journal of Nutrition* 130, no. 8 (2000), https://doi.org/10.1093/jn/130.8.2057S.
18. Lippi, "Chocolate in History: Food, Medicine, Medi-Food."
19. "History of Chocolate," History.com, December 14, 2017, https://www.history.com/topics/ancient-americas/history-of-chocolate#cacao-powder.
20. "History of Chocolate," History.com.
21. "Child Labor and Slavery in the Chocolate Industry," Food Empowerment Project, updated January 2022, https://foodispower.org/human-labor-slavery/slavery-chocolate/.
22. "Child Labor and Slavery," Food Empowerment Project.

23. "Bittersweet: Chocolate's Impact on the Environment," WWF, Spring 2017, https://www.worldwildlife.org/magazine/issues/spring-2017/articles/bittersweet-chocolate-s-impact-on-the-environment.

24. "Where to Find Fair-Trade Chocolate," Fair Trade Certified, October 17, 2023, https://www.fairtradecertified.org/blog/fair-trade-chocolate.

## Chapter 2: Chocolate by the Bite

1. Amy Guttman, "Real Life Willy Wonka Wins with Wild Flavors," *Forbes*, December 29, 2014, https://www.forbes.com/sites/amyguttman/2014/12/29/real-life-willy-wonka-wins-with-wild-flavors/.

2. Beyoncé et al., "Formation," *Lemonade*, 2016.

# Photo Credits

# Acknowledgments

I would like to express my heartfelt gratitude to the following individuals and groups whose contributions and support have made this cookbook possible:

First and foremost, I would like to thank God for the initial inspiration that set me on this culinary journey many years ago.

To my grandmother Jean; my mother, Arnettie; and my dad, Phil (Coach): for the knowledge and nurturing you have given me, I will forever be grateful. To the village of family members and friends, your support has meant the world to me.

To Werten Bellamy and Kellye Walker—two incredible individuals who have become family. Your unwavering support, encouragement, and belief in me since our first meeting have meant more than words can express. Thank you for being my champions, my sounding boards, and my constant sources of wisdom and inspiration. This journey would not have been the same without you. With deep gratitude and love, I dedicate this acknowledgment to you both.

I am incredibly grateful to my agent, Amy Hughes, and the talented publishing team at Harper Collins/Harper Celebrate. Their expertise, guidance, and dedication have been instrumental in bringing this cookbook to life.

A special thank you goes to Julie Tremaine, the exceptional collaborator who has gone above and beyond to ensure the accuracy and excellence of the recipes in this cookbook. Her feedback and suggestions have played a vital role in creating an incredible final product.

I would like to acknowledge the cacao farmers in West Africa who provide the finest quality beans that have been a constant source of inspiration for me. Their hard work and commitment to their craft have motivated me to make a positive impact on a global scale.

I extend my heartfelt appreciation to Juanita Slappy and the entire Cadillac team for their unwavering support throughout our journey together.

Lastly, I want to express my gratitude to the readers and home cooks who will be using this cookbook. Your enthusiasm and support serve as a constant inspiration for me to continue creating culinary masterpieces.

A special shout-out to Chef Jacques Torres for graciously contributing his words to this cookbook. Your involvement has truly elevated this project.

Thank you all for your contributions and support in bringing this cookbook to life.

# About the Author

**PHILLIP ASHLEY RIX** has achieved international acclaim as a renowned luxury chocolatier and is celebrated for his exceptional craftsmanship. He has created premium gifts for Hollywood's elite at the Emmys®, Grammys®, and Oscars®, and was named one of America's finest confectioners by *Forbes*. A finalist on Food Network's *Chopped Sweets*, his "Perfect Turtle" was featured on Oprah's Favorite Things list in 2020. He is the Official Chocolatier for Cadillac and was a James Beard Awards nominee in 2023 and 2024. His imaginative chocolate factory and home are in Memphis, Tennessee.

To learn more about Phillip, visit
www.phillipashley.com
@phillipashley